DIRECTIONS
FOR
CRITICISM
STRUCTURALISM
AND ITS ALTERNATIVES

DIRECTIONS
FOR
CRITICISM
STRUCTURALISM
AND ITS ALTERNATIVES

Edited by
Murray Krieger and L. S. Dembo

THE UNIVERSITY OF WISCONSIN PRESS

Published 1977
The University of Wisconsin Press
Box 1379, Madison, Wisconsin 53701

The University of Wisconsin Press, Inc.
70 Great Russell Street, London

First printing

Printed in the United States of America
ISBN 0-299-07390-4 cloth, 0-299-07394-7 paper
LC 77-77443

The articles in this volume originally appeared
in *Contemporary Literature*, Summer 1976

Contents

Prefatory Note

It has been almost a decade since *Contemporary Literature,* whose Summer 1976 issue we here offer in book form, devoted a number to modern criticism. Featuring a debate between Murray Krieger and Northrop Frye on interpretation and value judgment, with contributions by E. D. Hirsch and Wayne Shumaker, that early endeavor (Summer 1968) made its appearance in a world that was still three-dimensional or seemed so to most of us. Although the New Criticism had frequently been attacked, its assumptions about the integrity of the literary text and its methodology (explication) were still the alpha and omega of academic criticism in America. It was not until the seventies that the French *nouvelle critique* began to make a serious impression on critical thought in this country—that the fourth dimension opened up, and its creatures, begot by linguistics upon anthropology, could be seen on Main Street in broad daylight. (Actually, the first significant exposure to developments in France occurred in the fall of 1966 at the Johns Hopkins symposium on "The Languages of Criticism and the Sciences of Man," although the papers did not appear in book form until 1970.)

There remains even today some confusion over the trends that have been associated with a "new criticism." The members of the Geneva School—Marcel Raymond, Albert Béguin, Georges Poulet, Jean-Pierre Richard, Jean Starobinski, Jean Rousset, and Maurice Blanchot—were what Sarah N. Lawall called "the critics of consciousness" in her book so entitled (1968). They were interested chiefly in "a criticism of the author's experience conveyed in a text, and of his active consciousness at the moment of creation and perception." The structuralists per se, under the aegis of the linguists Ferdinand de Saussure and (later) Roman Jakobson and the cultural anthropologist Claude Lévi-Strauss, were concerned with defining the structures inherent in systems of signs, of which literature was only one among many (Roland Barthes, Tzvetan Todorov, Gérard Genette, et al.). Robert Scholes, in *Structuralism in Literature,* makes the point that structuralism is an affirmation of the mind's ability to know the world; that far from adhering to a philosophy of negation, it sees itself as a "human science" capable of identifying all the structures that make up a coherent universe. Its metaphysical antithesis can be found in a third group, called by Hayden White the Absurdists (Georges Bataille, Maurice Blanchot, Michel Foucault, Jacques Derrida, et al.), basically radical skeptics who, in denying the ability of "language" to express "reality," deny the validity of all forms of literary criticism and of knowledge in general. In light of the complexity of the subject, this brief sketch doesn't take us very far, but no matter. Scholes's introduction, lucid, sophisticated, and comprehensive, is readily available as is Jonathan Culler's *Structuralist Poetics* (1975), a masterpiece of exposition and original interpretation of the linguistic principles behind the movement and their application to literary theory.

Structuralism has found its converts and sympathizers in the U.S. but not among the contributors to this collection. Still, none of these scholars is a spokesman for the practical critic, who, either distrusting or uninterested in theory, continues to deal with the literary text as a self-contained object. Called "Normal" by Hayden White, the practical critic is clearly in the majority, if number of articles written for academic journals is any indication. For him, seeking theoretical alternatives to structuralism is as idle as pursuing the problems raised by structuralism itself. In other words, the problem is to find an alternative not to structuralism but to explication, which in being mass-produced has virtually reached a state of exhaustion.

Unfortunately, it is the very appearance on the American scene of French criticism, with its passion for technology and philosophic abstraction, that has, if anything, increased the horror of all theory among practical critics. Furthermore, the persistence of explication, despite the apparent disfavor into which the theories of the New Criticism have fallen, suggests that theory alone does not necessarily determine the kind of criticism that one writes, just as ethical systems are not directly translated into actual conduct.

Mr. Krieger, whose lifelong commitment to theory never needed stimulus from abroad, reveals his sensitivity to its weaknesses in the last paragraph of his introduction. He takes up the question at length in the opening chapter of his recently published *Theory of Criticism* (1976), conceding that theory is "prideful, even preening, in its glittering systematic displays and . . . ultimately—fruitless.'' This having been said, he argues that "literary theory, like it or not, must be faced: at whatever level of self-consciousness or sophistication, it is there for all readers of poetry; it is there, and ignoring it will not make it go away. Its inevitable presence derives from the fact that each of us carries with him, as he turns to experience a poem, some distillate of his earlier experiences of poems that acts as an a priori guide to his expectations, his interpretations, and his judgments. Conscious or unconscious, informed or uninformed, systematically worked out or ad hoc and piecemeal, this distillate still serves him, in effect, as his literary theory—even if it leads him to a disdain of the very notion of theory'' (pp. 5-6).

This is, of course, no defense of structuralism, and Krieger is most explicit about where he stands on the subject: "Having been one of those who fought in departments of literature to increase the importance accorded critical theory, I find it ironic that I am now concerned about its flourishing, out of my fear that in its recent forms [i.e., structuralism] theory leads away from the unique powers of literature as an art, the center of our humanistic domain'' (preface). What literary theory "can do for the criticism of specific works'' has always been for Krieger its main justification. This being the case, practical critics have nothing to fear from the creation at the University of California, Irvine, of the School of Criticism and Theory. Directed by Messrs. Krieger and Hazard Adams, it was for its first session (Summer 1976) staffed, with the exception of Edward Said, by the contributors to this collection. (The essays were written prior to this session and discussed at length in the course of it.) Far from giving structuralism an official institutional beachhead in this country, the School represents no *school* at all and, indeed, no unified viewpoint beyond its belief in the interchange and free play of theoretical conceptions.

A final note. Mr. Krieger is more than generous in his citation of my role in the creation of this collection. Overwhelmed by his (and Joan Krieger's) hospitality and benumbed by the stark beauty of the Irvine campus, which he was showing me when the matter came up, I doubtlessly would have agreed, had he proposed it, to devote a special issue of *Contemporary Literature* to the University of California catalogue—which is only to say that I played no part in the intellectual genesis of this volume. My subsequent editorial participation was to facilitate publication and attend to the burdensome and time-consuming details that editing any issue of the journal requires. In this I was aided by our managing editor, Linda Baker, whose penchant for accuracy involved us in a rigorous attention to style that was not above concerning itself with the ambiguities of comma usage and the like. Not exactly Structural Linguistics or Transformational Grammar (those "trinket pasticcios, flaunting skyey sheets"); no, no, just some practical editing that we hoped would end in "veracious page on page, exact."

                                                                    L. S. Dembo

February 1977

Acknowledgments

We are indebted to the University of Wisconsin Foundation, Rosa A. Pesta Estate, San Diego, California, for its assistance in producing the issue of *Contemporary Literature* (Summer 1976) in which the essays in this collection first appeared. We also wish to give special thanks to the following presses for providing the anthologies requested for each of the contributors: The University of Chicago Press; Cornell University Press; Dell Publishing Company; The Johns Hopkins University Press; and Little, Brown and Company.

Murray Krieger
L. S. Dembo

Contributors

MURRAY KRIEGER is University Professor of English at the University of California, teaching on the Irvine and Los Angeles campuses. Among his books are *The New Apologists for Poetry, The Play and Place of Criticism,* and *Theory of Criticism: A Tradition and Its System.* He is Co-Director of the newly founded School of Criticism and Theory at Irvine.

EDWARD W. SAID, Professor of English and Comparative Literature at Columbia University, has been a Fellow at the Center for Advanced Study in the Behavioral Sciences at Stanford for 1975-76. He is the author of *Joseph Conrad and the Fiction of Autobiography, Beginnings: Intention and Method,* and *Orientalism.*

HAZARD ADAMS has written books on Blake, Yeats, and literary theory as well as novels and poetry. A study on academic politics will appear this fall. He is currently Professor of English, University of Washington, Seattle, and Senior Fellow, School of Criticism and Theory at Irvine.

HAYDEN WHITE is Director of the Center for the Humanities at Wesleyan University and the author of *Metahistory* and several other books on intellectual history.

RENÉ GIRARD is James M. Beall Professor of French at Johns Hopkins University. His publications include *Mensonge romantique et vérité romanesque* and *La Violence et le sacré.*

RALPH FREEDMAN is completing a biography of Hermann Hesse and is the author of *The Lyrical Novel* as well as many critical studies on such writers as Valéry, Hesse, Coleridge, and Novalis. He is Professor of Comparative Literature at Princeton.

DIRECTIONS FOR CRITICISM
STRUCTURALISM AND ITS ALTERNATIVES

Introduction:
A Scorecard for the Critics

Murray Krieger

I remember, when I was a boy who attended baseball games with the frequency of an addict, that I used to resent the confident claim shouted by the vendors as they hawked their wares: "Buy a scorecard! Can't tell a player without a scorecard!" They seemed to be insisting that I needed to use their code book, which matched the numbers on the backs of the players' uniforms to their names, the positions they played, and their histories, before I could bestow any identity upon them. Such a minimal placement seemed contemptibly trivial and superficial to me, who had observed every idiosyncratic detail about the way each batter placed his feet and held and swung the bat, the way each pitcher prepared for and took his wind-up, the way each fielder took his position and moved for the ball. (Little did any of us know that history was to justify my impatience: some years later fans would be empowered to "tell a player" merely by reading his last name which was added to his number on the back of his uniform.)

There was another function which the scorecard was to serve. A system of minuscule boxes with diamond-shaped inserts next to the players' names permitted one, through the use of an elaborate baseball shorthand, to make a record of every play every inning. Thus the enthusiast could preserve—as he tried to create for himself—a unique historic occasion. But here, too, the scorecard frustrated me: in my anxiety to make my transcription detailed enough to jog my future memory with nuance as well as with the crude abstraction of consequences, I continually overran the boxes, extending my coded markings until they produced a jumbled mass

3

on a page where no blank space remained to separate the individual actions or the actions grouped into individual innings. All that remained legible, in the end, was the coarsest reduction of all—the cold numbers isolated at the bottom of the page reporting, for each inning, the runs, hits, and errors. In the end I was as exasperated with myself as with the scorecard—as much with my incapacity to accept the need to discriminate and to omit as with the procedure that made it necessary for me to do so. It may have been true that everything really counted, but it was also true that the scorecard ritual required that less than everything be recorded. Some placement of the players, their actions, and the consequences of those actions for the team and the game was needed, though the nominal labels that went with the numbers on their backs hardly characterized the players any more than the rude numbering of their runs, hits, and errors constituted that delicately maneuvered game they played. So, despite the inadequacies that troubled the observations of a self-confessed expert witness, the scorecard process—however misleading here and there—was a helpful and not altogether inaccurate one.

I make this personal recital because I see this essay as having something of a scorecard function—of placing (if not labeling) our critics and trying to keep count of their runs, hits, and errors—and I see myself as probably the wrong man to play the scorecard-keeper's role. When Professor Dembo asked me to organize and act as editor for this number of *Contemporary Literature*, we conceived it as a kind of scorecard to track the varieties of recent criticism. However, to the extent that this conception was realized, it becomes my task, in this introductory essay, to keep score of the scorekeepers. If each of them felt licensed to judge as well as to observe, to press forward certain attitudes toward literature and its criticism at the expense of others—in short, to be polemic as well as descriptive—it is clear that my position as scorekeeper-once-removed requires me to be more restrained. This need for me to suppress my own preferences and to resist climbing into the theoretical arena is the more oppressive in view of the fact that I have just completed a book (to appear at just about the same time as this issue) whose title, *Theory of Criticism*, should not mask the parochialism of its commitments. Still, I have tried to permit that work to remain the repository of my partisanship for this moment, as I have struggled toward a disinterested transcendence in playing my role here. Like Pope's dispassionately rational God, I was to see "with equal eye" the making and unmaking of systematic worlds and bubbles: in short, the scorecard-keeper was to replace the partisan fan. Since this is a difficult role for mortal man to play—especially for me, especially at this time—I felt it necessary to warn the reader of this additional disqualification which I bring with me to my task, one for which my irritation with labeling and generalized defining already renders me unfit.

It occurred to Professor Dembo and me that our theoretical spectrum these days was in considerable need of whatever demarcations could be made within its graded variations by knowing and intelligent observer-participants. The classifier of methodologies could look back nostalgically at the simplicity of his problems in the limited warfare only a few decades back among New Critics, biographical and historical scholars, neo-humanists, neo-Aristotelians, and old-style Freudians and Marxists. How much more problematic these days are the challenges and cross-challenges not only to critical method but to the very assumption that there is an object or a language for criticism, as we move through the baffling array of structuralisms, post-structuralisms, and phenomenologies, as well as the still-lingering versions of older positions now modified to confront these revolutionary alternatives, largely continental, which could not have been anticipated even a short while back. So we thought any effort toward classification and commentary would be useful, although all my skepticism from my scorecard-keeping days warned me that, given a complexity in which almost everything was constituted by differences and difference itself was elevated to a principle both metaphysical and antimetaphysical, such an effort—in its necessary simplifications—would be misleading as well. But we still decided to try, proposing to call the joint effort *Directions for Criticism: Structuralism and Its Alternatives*.

Our selection of theorists was meant to display a variety of methodological commitments and areas of humanistic and literary interest—at least as much variety as one could reasonably expect from only five authors whom we also wanted to be distinguished commentators on theory and makers of theory. Since at much the same time we at Irvine were organizing a Board of Senior Fellows for our planned School of Criticism and Theory, basing the selection on much the same criteria, it should hardly be surprising to find that our authors are members of that Board. Regarded in this light, our collection of essays here has another and more immediate function: it serves to delineate the current situation in critical theory against which any such institution must measure its mission. Since that institution is just now in its first summer session, the appearance of this journal is most timely, and the writing of these essays for it has been an appropriate way to prepare to guide the work of the School.

Once our authors were chosen, there had to be a fictive occasion created to stimulate them to produce studies that would reflect on one another and on the state of criticism. I therefore projected a make-believe symposium: we would suppose ourselves seated around an imaginary table, on which we found a number of anthologies which have collected, according to various principles of selection, recent essays in critical theory. Then each of our authors would react to issues raised by them, and I would try to group their reactions. Even though there are obvious shortcomings in anthologies (such as have been pointed out in the essays that follow), it seemed wise to me to avoid the sort of squabbles over critical personalities and the hierarchy among them that might ensue if I chose books by a limited number of arbitrarily chosen theorists. Better to have an arbitrary choice of anthologies, with their arbitrary choices of essays or chapters of books, in the hope that, among them all, enough representative work would be assembled to produce significant responses in our authors. So, with the cooperation of the publishers, the following books were distributed:

In Search of Literary Theory, ed. Morton W. Bloomfield (Ithaca: Cornell Univ. Press, 1972).

European Literary Theory and Practice: From Existential Phenomenology to Structuralism, ed. Vernon W. Gras (New York: Dell, 1973).

The Languages of Criticism and the Sciences of Man: The Structuralist Controversy, ed. Richard Macksey and Eugenio Donato (Baltimore: Johns Hopkins Press, 1970).

Velocities of Change: Critical Essays from MLN, ed. Richard Macksey (Baltimore: Johns Hopkins Univ. Press, 1974).

Issues in Contemporary Literary Criticism, ed. Gregory T. Polletta (Boston: Little, Brown and Co., 1973).

Modern French Criticism: From Proust and Valéry to Structuralism, ed. John K. Simon (Chicago: Univ. of Chicago Press, 1972).

As will be apparent in the essays that follow, we did not solicit mere surveys or reviews: there was no requirement or even suggestion that the entire spectrum of work represented in these anthologies be responded to, or that the issues arousing the response be broad rather than narrow, shared by many rather than by a few. We hoped for a distribution and breadth of focus. But mainly there was the hope that each of our essayists would find something or many somethings that would provoke him to contribute to our awareness and our understanding of questions currently seeking responsive gestures from those helping to shape where criticism is and is going. Whether stimulated by a wide array of essays, authors, and theoretical positions, or by just one (or by anything in between), each was to use that as his point of origin leading to some more general observation about the state and the tendencies of the theory around us. Unfortunately, circumstances prevented us from allowing for any interaction among our five major authors, so that each essay stands independently of the others, neither reflected in them nor reflecting upon them. Nevertheless, I claim to find areas of debate among them in my essay, the only one written after the others and in reaction to what they were doing. Hence I try to restrict my reactions to them instead of reacting on my own to the anthologies. If my remarks alone have the advantage of being a response to those of my colleagues, then I must be the more restrained, taking care to maintain the disinterestedness I find so hard to cultivate. It is also true that, just as the completed scorecard can normally be seen only after the game has been played, my comments should perhaps be read after, rather than before, the five essays. But there is an introductory function to be served here also, as I search for a structure of dialogue that can contain as well as place them in advance.

I shall proceed in the most obvious way, dealing with our five authors one at a time, beginning with those who survey the widest field of issues and theorists and moving to those who concentrate on just a few specific problems and writers. But in the end none is narrow in the consequences he draws from his observations. Further, none is merely a reporter, all are argumentative; but the centers toward which their arguments gather differ in the range of current critical practice they encompass. Edward Said and Hazard Adams come to very different conclusions about a large collection of critics and writings in these volumes: they do not agree about how to group them or, more important, how to judge those groupings. Hayden White is most concerned about the post-structuralist theorists, although he still cuts a very wide swathe among them—and others he discusses by way of contrast. René Girard seems to draw his argument exclusively out of his concern with Lévi-Strauss, except that his conclusions spread out to affect our view of structuralism and post-structuralism, as well as of his own quite original alternative. And Ralph Freedman restricts his interest to the phenomenological tradition in criticism though he ends with wider and more ambitious claims.

I

Edward Said seeks to provide historical placement both for recent critical schools and for individual critics whose common interests often blur the apparent differences in the schools that are sometimes seen as claiming them as members. For his interest in placement is subordinated to his interest in returning literature (as well as criticism itself) to its social nexus. Indeed, so anxious does he appear to return literature to the historical and social dynamics which give it its shape that he broadens the common attack upon the formalism of the New Criticism to include mainline structuralism within its range.

Early in his essay, he marks off the *new* new criticism (mainly continental criticism) by its rejection of the mere "object-ness" of "a confined text," which we usually associate with the old New Criticism—a claim with which many would readily enough agree. But, despite this claim, he argues that in "most of the anthological materials" we "will find the critic talking about what a text does, how it works, how it has been put together in order to do certain things, how the text is a wholly integrated and equilibrated system." In view of the obvious fact that our anthologies are post-New Critical and heavily continental in their inclusions, we may well find this observation a baffling one. Said properly traces this attitude toward the text back to "the advent of American and English New Criticism," a "functionalist criticism" that grows out of "a rigorous technical vocabulary based mainly upon linguistic terminology" which, in later critics, sharpens itself at the expense of the poem, "since one aim of functionalism is to perfect the instrument of analysis as much as one's understanding of a text's workings." Surprisingly, the next example of such functionalism is Barthes, latest proponent of the "critical ingenuity" that transposes "the work—any work—into an instance of the method."

Said finds that critical ingenuity—and arrogance—that can create common cause among writers from the old New Critics to Barthes is rooted in their need to center and isolate "the text." If he now claims such alliances, then, as I have suggested, it is difficult to reconcile this common commitment to a text and its functioning with Said's earlier claim that recent continental criticism is marked by its turning from the text as its object, rather seeing the object elide itself by sliding into an activity. Yet he mainly—at least in the cited passages—prefers to ignore this major difference between those committed to literature as object and those committed to literature as activity: he rather comes to group together philologians, New Critics, and structuralists (his "constellation" includes Auerbach, Spitzer, Blackmur, Barthes, Genette, and Benjamin, and he will add Frye and even Poulet), seeing them all as readers "whose learning is *for* the text, and whose method is *from* the text." He must surely grant the great differences among them in their notions about what a text is—some restricting the privilege to literary fictions and others broadening it to an indiscriminate coverage of *écriture*—but above such differences he holds their common concern for "how language signifies, what it signifies, and in what form." (Though Said has shrewd strategic reasons for his groupings, one might wonder how comfortable the structuralist would be with a characterization that has him as concerned with "signifieds" as with "signifiers." Or one might wonder how much Poulet's commitment to a fluid consciousness would have to be altered before it could be fastened to a fixed object, a text.)

The motive for Said's exaggerated effort to find common ground among so motley a group is his theoretical need to find an alternative to their centering attention upon a text. By lining up these varied voices he thinks he can expose what he sees as their similar neglect of social forces, first, because they are devoted exclusively to the text as a privileged document and, second, because they fail to root such texts—as well as their own work—in the historical realities that feed and shape them. Thus he clears the way to proposing another group of critics as antidotes to such elitist oversight.

Since Said echoes the frequent complaint uttered by different people at different times against both structuralists and New

Critics—that they are ahistorical, gaining the synchronic only by denial of the diachronic—he can introduce, among others, Foucault and Bloom (or, as parallel cases, Schwab and Bate) as exemplary figures who seek to restore literature to its place as part of our social reality in time. The dynamic restlessness of existential sequence, through such as these, sweeps over the text, making it part of its own continuity, submerging all contours. While Said acknowledges that such a notion of literary history makes it exclusively a continuous unfolding, an unbroken linearity of dramatic change, and while he therefore concedes the need for some balancing notions of "stabilities," structured in repetitions and in cultural institutions, he clearly feels that the change in emphasis is so necessary that even such excesses are welcome. For in contrast to the "worldless" criticism he rejects, this criticism is "about, and indeed is, the text's situation in the world."

Here again, with Foucault and Bloom, Said—as he concedes— has created a strange alliance. Between the two there is the difference between a historical concern that sees all discourse struggling to find itself as part of the culture's archive and a historical concern that sees all poems struggling to create themselves out of opposition to, and in competition with, the earlier poems that seek to determine them. Bloom is unlike Foucault in that he sees antagonism rather than cooperation between text and archive, but also in that his archive is a literary one: he dwells on the special sort of familial relations between a poet's text and those of his poet-ancestors rather than on the uniform relations between texts of whatever sort and the collective system they make up.

This latter difference may well remind us of the difference we remarked earlier between structuralists and New Critics—between the dedication to a text as part of *écriture* and the dedication to a literary text as a uniquely aesthetic entity. One might well view Bloom and the New Critics, however great their differences, allied (against Foucault and the structuralists) as literary devotees concerned about those who would deny them a specially discernible object, while on their side Foucault and the structuralists might bury their differences long enough to assail any such attempt to lift poetry out of the common domain of discourse on the assumption that it required distinctive treatment. These pairings may seem no more difficult to establish (if no less so) than Said's cross-pairings. That he insists on making his, in spite of the internal differences that undercut them, is indicative of his exclusive concentration on the need to return literature and its criticism to their places in the world of action. So he concentrates on the common historical commitments of Foucault and Bloom that distinguish them from structuralists and New Critics, respectively. The two work in their different but equally history-conscious ways to deny the text's presence by dissolving it into the no-longer-absent past. It is this notion, Said's argument reminds us, that permits Bloom to find a community of interest with post-structuralist continental theory.

Thus Said calls for a concern with what we used to term the sociology of literature, an interest in such extraliterary circumstances as condition every element of a text from its beginnings to its currency with readers at one moment and its neglect at another. (Said exemplifies his own precept in his recently published volume, *Beginnings: Intention and Method*.) Those familiar with the criticism of this past century may well view as a return to old-fashioned pre-New Critical enquiries such investigations into linguistic, social, and cultural history as sources for the creation of a work or investigations into the circumstances that—after the work has been created—make or unmake its reputation. But Said argues that Foucault's archeology provides for the renewal of such studies within an original and productive framework.

More significantly, Said extends his plea for worldliness from an active role seen for literature to an active role seen for criticism itself. He summons criticism not only to treat literature as a social act, but to join literature by itself being undertaken as a social act. He thus willfully blurs criticism and literature in accordance with his own doctrine of an unprivileged *écriture*, one that enacts its social role through the text, trying to win freedom *for* society instead of freedom *from* it. So the critic has this as his independent obligation—independent, that is, of the text. He is to act in his own behalf: his work is to be conceived as an action in the world.

Said welcomes, as the consequence of such a notion, the claim that criticism is in competition with the literary text as an original act, that it has its beginnings in itself—that, in short, it is constitutive and sovereign rather than derivative and subservient. He speaks with some contempt, then, of the "simplistic opposition between originality and repetition" that holds for most critics who bow in humility before their object. As in all writing, he asserts, criticism should begin by creating its object, not by finding it. Tradi-

tional criticism forgoes "independent creation in criticism" because of
naively realistic assumptions that lead it to mythologize the literary
work into an object before which it modestly submits, as secondary submits to primary. Said's doctrine of universal autotelism in
writing, all devoted to becoming modes of action, may seem to fly
in the face of the critic's conventional common sense of his
relation to the poem—of his very *raison d'être*—but it follows
logically, even necessarily, from the denial of a privileged status to
literature and the granting of an equal place for all writing in our
culture's archive. The denial to criticism of its external object is of
a piece with the denial of objects to all writing (including what we
used to term literature or *poesis*). It appears to reflect the structuralist's insistence that no signifieds exist for the empty signifiers
which we choose to turn into any kind of writing we address
(though self-deceptively) to any object (or to whatever we reify
into an object).

But criticism for Said, having a historical commitment, must
go where structuralists disdain to go—into the world of time to
make itself felt. Toward those he sees as critics centered on the
text—structuralists, New Critics, or other nonactivists—Said feels his
own disdain: "Contemporary criticism achieved its methodological
independence by forfeiting an active situation in the world. It has
no faith in traditional continuities (nation, biography, period);
rather it improvises, in acts of an often inspired *bricolage*, order
out of extreme discontinuity. Its culture is a negative one of
absence, anti-representation, and (as Blackmur used to put it
repeatedly) ignorance." Thus Said constructs an archeological
placement for this criticism, accounting for it by showing its
negative relation to the world. He has performed in accordance
with the alternative criticism he proposes—one that would find,
within a unified historical field, continuities among writings which,
in constituting themselves and their objects, also constitute a cultural archive. Free from a world of objects, such criticism—as an
equal among those writings—yet leads us to the world as it takes
its place in it.

II

Hazard Adams, as an observer of the contemporary critical
scene reflected in the anthologies, is a self-conscious partisan for

the kind of criticism Edward Said rejects. But, as we should expect, he shifts the philosophical ground to one which, in supporting him, would force the collapse of the structure of recent continental thought. He views "the so-called crisis of language" imposed upon us by this thought as one in which "criticism threatens to break down all boundaries and to rival (by obliteration) literature itself." This is an apt description of a central assumption of Said's essay. In words that echo the mood of that essay, Adams complains that "the critic seems tempted to compete with his texts, to surpass them, and in his most ebullient moods . . . to deny the existence of literature entirely." But this is the very critic Said hopefully invoked, so that he would hardly take Adams' words as a charge to be answered. (Curiously, Said complained that such critics were more to be invoked for the future than presently to be seen, while Adams observes them in large and influential numbers.) From the opposite perspective, Adams is quite willing to place himself among those who express "profound respect for the unmeasurable distance between criticism and the poem"—the very attitude which Said saw as "simplistic" in its relegation of criticism to the role of a distant and inadequate attendant to the poem.

Indeed, the argument that grows out of Adams' observations springs entirely from his sense of this distance which Said denies— the awesome gap he points out between criticism and the poem which is its object. From the beginning Adams emphasizes (citing arguments in Vico and Cassirer) that the philosopher's language makes it difficult to speak of poetic or mythic thinking "from its own point of view," "from inside itself." Adams continues, "The problem with respect to poetry is the same as that with myth: even the most careful of discursive approaches betrays an alien perspective." If this distance between poetic discourse and the critic's discourse about it depends on a sense of the difference in the language of the two entities, then what must follow is the claim that the poem is a most privileged discourse. Yet Adams is very cautious in making this claim, even at times coming close to rescinding it. For he is aware of the indefensibility of an absolute distinction between poetic and "normal" or "ordinary" uses of language, just as he is aware that the notion of a baldly referential, normal discourse is an unreal fiction. So whatever the critic must say about the poem as a privileged discourse, with a special power for radical creation in language, he must say with an irony that bears within it a sense of mere fiction. Yet, in contrast to Said, for Adams the text is primary—and a poetic text at that.

Adams cannot launch his theoretical counterattack upon continental theoretical fashions without assaulting head-on the omnibus conception of language in accordance with signifier-signified analysis. And it is both the analysis, and the fact that it is indiscriminately applied to all language, that he finds open to challenge, a challenge launched by the humanist against a threatened intrusion by a positivism dominated—consciously or otherwise—by the perspective of the social sciences. The opposition between signifier and signified, as Adams views it, can occur only within a crudely and archaically mimetic notion about how language functions, with its signs pointing to things or concepts; and he finds this true even of the structuralists who, having made the analysis, go on to claim that there are really only signifiers, making patterns among one another, since all apparent signifieds are the product of our mythologizing reification. If such be the case, then all language represents the futile effort to capture a ˅world that forever eludes it. It is not a long step from here for Adams to account for Paul de Man's notion of poetic allegory as the dominant mode for the romantic poet as ironist—the acknowledgment of the failure of the poem's words to leap across the distance that separates them from the things they would enclose. The poet's consciousness of his empty signifiers leads him to make his poem the representative utterance of the structuralist limitations upon all our language.

Adams sees the sign-thing or sign-concept dichotomy for all language as resting upon a naive epistemology that ignores all that we have known since Kant (if not Vico), and he sees the sign-thing or sign-concept dichotomy as especially disabling when we try to speak of poetic creation in language. For him the poetic is representative of the inherently creative capacity of all language. This is to say that Adams can conceive of "the idea of language as creative of such *signifié* as it has," as he seeks, "borrowing from Vico and Cassirer," "a theory of radical creativity in language that gives priority to the poetic." He projects a language continuum moving from a "poetic center" "outward through the zone of ordinary language" to a "mathematic circumference." The monistic heart of the word-making process reveals the creative principle that is central to all language usage, even if—as we often witness and participate in it—it has degenerated toward the passivity of a deadly dualism. He thus denies the norm of an ordinary pointer-language (with its sign-referent dualism), from which poetic language would represent a deviation, arguing instead for the centrality of the poetic as the vital creative norm from which all else is a falling off. Language is constitutive of its world, even—alas—when, using its dying elements, we create only a dull world with it.

Can such a continuum support the opposition between poetic and ordinary language which Adams sometimes seems to need even though his epistemology requires him to reject it? When we ask whether or not Adams believes in an opposition between poetry and ordinary language, we find two answers. First, he must deny it at the theoretical level: as poetry is the central human way of speech and writing (being logically—and perhaps even historically—prior, in the manner of Vico and Shelley as well as Cassirer), all less-creative speech and writing are gradations away from it. So, "from its own point of view," "from inside itself," the answer is that there can be no such opposition. But secondly, he must allow it in the back door as a practical necessity for the unpoetic critic: as he, with his fallen language, talks of poetry from his "alien perspective," he must create the fiction (with an ironic self-consciousness about that fictional status) that the poetry-nonpoetry opposition appears to criticism to exist. It is, consequently, in this sense that we can speak of allegory as the critic's method of describing what, from inside the poem, is a symbolic unity. Here is the ground of his argument with de Man: the distance which de Man claims to find between the poetic word and its object Adams claims really exists only between the critic's word and the poet's. For the poet's word is creator and container of its object for Adams, so that the allegory is not the poet's (as with de Man), but the critic's.

It would seem, then, that Adams will admit a phenomenological opposition between poetry and ordinary language (which includes the critic's language), while denying on epistemological and even metaphysical grounds that such an opposition—or even a concept like ordinary language—can exist. "It is necessary here to state that the theory of radical creativity, though it refuses to draw a line *measuring off* poetry from other forms of discourse and argues for the creativity of all language, does not quarrel with our needs as critics to create an ironic fictive opposition where a continuum is the reality." Adams is aware that such a claim (and we must note his giveaway term "reality") has ontological implications and is thus vulnerable to continental demystification, the dissolving of his myth of origins. One may, I think, properly wonder whether he needs the Viconian or Blakean epistemology in order to make his phenomenological—his fictive and ironic—claim. One may wonder also what advantage he gains as a theorist of literary criticism to insist metaphysically on a continuum, when poetry looks upon itself from within, in view of his admission of discontinuities and oppositions, when poetry is looked upon by the critic from outside, which is the only side from which he can look or speak.

What remains important about Adams' position, as we see it distinguished from Said's, is the insistence that, under the poetic dispensation (whether seen as universally constitutive or as constitutive only within verbal works of art), words be treated as symbols rather than as signs, that signifiers be seen not as empty but as full of the signifieds that they create in order to contain. Such words, of course, cannot be viewed as "worldless"—which is how Said claimed modern text-oriented critics viewed them. Adams thus reminds us that, in lumping all text-oriented critics together, Said failed to distinguish those who saw words as cut off from the world from those who saw words as opening us up to the world. Adams would claim that his way of focusing on the text leads to our apprehension of the world it constitutes. Such are the far-flung theoretical consequences of his anti-structuralist refusal to start with a concept of language based on signifiers at a distance from, and only arbitrarily related to, their signifieds.

Thus Adams can, on *his* grounds, join Said in pleading for a criticism that helps make it possible for both literature and itself to play a historical and anthropological role. But Adams would complain not only about structuralists as "worldless" but also about diachronic critics like de Man (or, might he add, Said?) who—despite their distance from structuralism—are like structuralists trapped by the binary opposition between signifier and signified and by the positivistic assumptions which make that opposition a monolithic one. Hence they cannot, like him, show how truly world-ful the poem can be. Adams joins in the Goethean "insistence on the poet's connection with the concrete and particular, with earth. . . . Goethe does verge on asserting a positive cultural role for poetry, moving from the negative enclosure of the Faustian study to establishment of the poetic power, not of transcendence, but of building on earth, presumably in language."

Adams similarly rejects the "negative enclosure" of the structuralist view of language. As if answering Said's call, though in alien terms that lead him in directions which Said would prefer to shut off, Adams sees the word, like the human poem it constitutes, "as potentially creative of cultural reality, which is of the earth, but an earth of man's making and remaking in symbolic form."

III

The differences I have been marking in the positions of Said and Adams are accounted for in Hayden White's ambitious historical undertaking, which attempts to place all the varied phases of recent literary theory, relating them to one another and to the culture that both produced them and determined when they would come into and go out of fashion. Adams and Said are surely worthy representatives of White's "Normal" critic and "Absurdist" critic, respectively. With the historian's transcendent dispassion, White traces the several moments of each, as the two wrestle for dominance of the contemporary critical scene. The "Normal" critic holds the traditional view that criticism can illuminate the meaning of a text and assess its value; and such a criticism assumes the possibility of literature—of a literary text that contains such a meaning and value. On the other hand, the "Absurdist" critic at the least calls both literature and, therefore, criticism into question and at the most denies the possibility of either to exist as containers of meaning.

While it is obvious what makes the first group "Normal," White argues for the second as "Absurdist" on the ground that they write and continue to write "at interminable length and *alta voce*" about "the virtues of silence": they "criticize endlessly in defense of the notion that criticism is impossible." Such reflexive contradiction constitutes a position that "is manifestly Absurd." But if the absurd "is simply that which cannot be thought," when someone like Derrida "not only thinks the unthinkable but turns it into an idol," he is "Absurdist." Finding the source of Absurdism in Paulhan, Bataille, Blanchot, and Heidegger, White sees it carried "to its logical conclusion" in Foucault, Barthes, and Derrida. And it is clear that he would find Said's definition of the critic's plight and opportunity—as I have observed it—well within his Absurdist camp. On the other side, Adams would be for him a splendid summoner to a return to critical normalcy. Indeed, White would see him not only as "Normal," but as representative of the most fetishizing subgroup of the "Normal"—the "Inflationary" critics.

Perhaps I should trace briefly the several subgroups of these two general tendencies which White gathers into a dramatic parade of critical fashions from the latter part of the last century until today—with the unhistorical implication that there may be no tomorrow. The first version of "Normal" criticism, as its practice comes into the twentieth century through the First World War, he terms "Elementary" criticism. It moves out of a naive acceptance of the function of criticism to discover and communicate textual meanings and aesthetic value and, by doing so, advances culture and civilization. The privileged status of literature is thus assumed, although the untroubled process of criticism precludes mystery. A countermovement arises between the wars—"Reductive" criticism—spawned by the new would-be social sciences (Marxism, psychoanalysis, sociology of knowledge) and devoted to stripping the text down to its "hidden, more basic, and preliterary content," to merge literature with "life." It thus springs from an anti-elitist impulse but is still "Normal" in that it does not question the capacity of literature to hold meanings and of criticism to uncover them.

Yet another reaction asserts itself, producing in the post-Second-World-War years a newer version of "Elementary" criticism, but this time self-consciously theoretical and defensive, having learned the hard lessons imposed by the "Reductive" ascendancy. What emerges is a third variety, "Inflationary" criticism, an alliance (despite differences) among New Critics, "practical" critics (White cites Leavis and Trilling), and "formal" critics (he cites Frye), dedicated to literature as little less than a sacred object embodying "high culture" in its transformation of mere life. Its "objective" methods were to bring "Normal" criticism to a new completeness. (We can see at once that Hazard Adams fits the "Inflationary" category very well.) We are ripe, at this point, for another reaction against an autotelic and privileged notion of art, and the existentialist critics, like Sartre and Camus, provide it. But this time, as art is related (and perhaps reduced) to human need, as it was earlier by "Reductive" critics, its very existence—like that of criticism—is brought into doubt. The problematic of literature and of criticism enters our scene for the first time. And we are ready for this problematic to be systematically—indeed, even programmatically—

pursued in our next variety, "Generalized" criticism, as jointly developed by phenomenological and structuralist theorists. Criticism is generalized in that literature becomes no more than a part of language-in-general, which is a universal system of signs, a uniform (if uniformly inadequate) projection of consciousness. Both literature and criticism are first blurred and then lost in a unified field theory. What remains is the final stage, "Absurdist" criticism, which dares to take the consequences of such "arbitrary" workings of an empty language system and, thus, to accept the reflexive impossibilities of both the poetic and the critical act.

Yet, in this final reversal of "Inflationary" criticism, mystique returns, in whatever negative guise. White calls our attention to Said's acknowledgment that, for the structuralist, "everything is a text ... or ... nothing is a text." But in the discussion that follows, White seems to replace the "or" with an "and," making it clear that, for the Absurdist, both possibilities are maintained at once. As a consequence, " 'the act of reading' could become fetishized, turned into a mystery which is at once a fascinating and at the same time cruelly mutilating activity." Such paradox is cause of a further one: the denial of privilege to any text does not prevent the implicit claim that there are privileged readers, with access to the mystery of all and/or nothing, and to the complicated discourse in which such mystery is set forth and discussed. And this becomes yet another paradox: such tortuous discourse revolves endlessly about a subject whose very existence it precludes. Yet, despite or because of the cultivation of such paradoxes, here is where—for White—criticism now finds itself, strongly backed by current intellectual fashion.

The very trimness of White's scheme, which finds one critical fashion replacing another at center stage, naturally invites the claim that the errant facts surrounding the actual work of theorists and groups of theorists are in some instances at odds with the design of his chronicle. These are the necessary risks the historian must run if he has the courage and the largeness of vision to undertake the organization of such resistant and complex data. For example, it is not altogether accurate to portray the New Critics as reacting to the Reductive critics and reviving—in more sophisticated form—the literary devotion of the Elementary. One might argue that they were at least as much a reaction against Elementary critics, like the so-called impressionists and neo-humanists and historical scholars, as the Reductive critics were. Indeed, it may be that the New Critics

were more anxious to react against such Elementary critics
than they were to react against the Reductive critics. White would
thus have to move back his placement of this variety of Inflationary criticism to well before the Second World War, seeing it in
the thirties as being as much an extra-academic movement as he
found the Reductive critics to be.

Or again, it is hardly likely that existentialist critics like Sartre
or Camus were aware enough of Inflationary critics of the sort
White deals with for them to come into being as a reaction against
Inflationary criticism. Nor is the relative timing of the two movements such as to support a cause-and-effect relationship between
them. But White needs the anti-Inflationary consequences of
existentialism in order to move toward the anti-elitism of his
Generalized critics—the phenomenologists and structuralists he
views as post-existentialist. Further, his attempted union between
phenomenologists and structuralists forces him to join the primary
interest in "human consciousness" to the primary interest in a
"universe of speech acts" as if they were one interest, when the
antagonism between the two groups stems from the fact that they
can be opposed interests. Thus, as we have noticed before—for
example, in dealing with Said—a special way of viewing the schools
of critics and the drama played among them requires the marshal-
ling of groupings that may, from alien perspectives, seem difficult
to defend. (We can recall that, whereas Said grouped Barthes with
Spitzer and Blackmur, White groups him with Derrida and Foucault—and that White sees these last two theorists as mutually
reinforcing while Said set them against one another.)

There is another risk that the historian must take as he
constructs the cause-and-effect pattern out of which his story
emerges. When we review White's drama of this sequence of critical
moments in a rapid-fire summary such as mine has been, we find
that he has imposed several shaping structures to control that
sequence, perhaps to overdetermine it. He sees the causal relations
between one critical moment and the next turn into a repetitive
pattern of reaction, counterreaction, and then yet another reaction
that is the first one returned in a more sophisticated form, thanks
to the lessons of the second—and so on. It is something of a
Hegelian succession—a method of description strangely at odds
with the decentered way the succession ends (though the notion of
a decentered ending is self-contradictory). What is suggested is a
series of linked and opposed movements and a systolic-diastolic

rhythm established by them. The Elementary and the Inflationary critical modes are interlaced with the Reductive and the Generalized modes in a sequence in which the idolatry of art alternates with the desire to demythologize and level it. Naiveté breeds reduction, reduction breeds inflation, inflation breeds egalitarianism. But also, fetish breeds fetish: Absurdism, the fifth moment, has echoes within it of both ally and antagonist, being a "fetishization" of the structuralism it succeeds and yet—as a fetishization—answering the counterfetishization of the poetic object in Inflationary criticism. So echoes are either of similar critical values or of similar critical dispositions at the service of opposed values.

The rhythm has been kept moving by the repetitive principle of reaction, so that each movement is seen as calling forth its answering opponent-successor. In effect, each movement gets what it had coming to it, and all of us and our culture get what we have had coming to us as Absurdism becomes history's vengeance upon us: "In Absurdist criticism, the dualism of Western thought and the elitism of Western social and cultural practice come home to roost." Since dualism and its consequent elitism have, White acknowledges, been with us since Plato, "this Absurdist moment was potentially present from the beginning of modern European humanism." The previous critical moments of ours which he has traced, however seemingly resistant, are the final avenues to the Absurdist apocalypse we have been building toward: "Now dualism is hypostatized as the condition of Being-in-general and meaninglessness is embraced as a goal. And elitism is stood on its head."

So the historical rhythm does more than just alternate. It has an objective, however destructive: as the revolutionary answer to the hierarchical habit of an obsolete society, it means to undo an elitist cultural tradition. We may begin to sense that, as he has constructed this anti-teleology, our historian has been complicitous with his history in leaving us where he does, however unhappy he may claim to be about it. The cool dispassion which distances his pain helps disguise the extent to which he has been in control of the drama. We must remember also that he further justifies this perverse revenge, which our culture has asked for and has had visited upon it, by pointing to our gross economic reduction of all things to an equivalence of mere "commodities." Thus all our cherished notions of value must now be seen as myths which our culture has fraudulently used to disguise the egalitarian march of familiar signifiers. It is appropriate, White suggests, that our criticism, in its primary concern with value, should now level all our precious objects to the "arbitrary" indiscriminateness of the commodity economy. (One may wonder whether, in attempting to account for the emergence of Absurdism by applying such economic metaphors to the critical realm, he may himself be joining the Reductive critics whom he placed some decades back.) The undiscriminating commitment to arbitrariness in our culture is, for White, a major force in the triumph of Saussurian linguistics, with its arbitrary relation between signifier and signified which we have seen Adams reject and White deplore. But, given the implied determinism of White's scheme, he cannot join Adams in trying to conceive for our art a language whose creativity would permit it, as signifier, to constitute its signifieds in and through its very form, thus converting the arbitrary into the inevitable. For this would suggest a privileged sanctuary for language which the economic metaphors that shape our culture would preclude. Better the Absurdism, whatever the blankness of its vision, as the fitting deconstruction of the monstrosities we have constructed.

It is not surprising that White feels required to end by admitting, despairingly, that the questions of the Absurdists "put the Normal critics in the position of having to provide answers which they themselves cannot imagine." The questions sustain all the levels of the reflexive problematic that—short of contradiction—should have precluded the Absurdists from asking them. How, possessed as they are of a more-than-arbitrary commitment to language, can Normal critics imagine answers to questions which presuppose a reflexive problematic, one that precludes the possibility of their ever having been asked—even by Absurdists? Such is the box in which White sees them enclosed (or in which he has enclosed them). For, as so often happens with daringly ambitious historians, it is difficult to tell whether the box is his or history's.

White's apocalypse reaches out from the history of literature and its criticism to enclose our entire culture, our world itself. He partly fixes the blame for this extension on Derrida who, guilty of what Frye called "existential projection," "fetishizes" the structuralists' dualism "and treats [their poles of language] as the fundamental categories of Being." But partly too, we have seen, it is the guilt of our culture itself which invites the Absurdist conception of language to destroy not only its poetry but its very being as a meaningful construct. As Pope, in the apocalyptic close of *The Dunciad*, reached beyond his grim picture of the contemporary

literary world to envision the fearful destruction of the contemporary world itself, so White seems to end by shrinking from what
he has justified. In Pope's language, under the burden of the
"uncreating word," "universal darkness buries all."

IV

Others, of course (we may think at once of Edward Said), will
agree with White about the revolutionary implications and consequences—both literary and cultural—of post-structuralist thinking
without sharing his dark view of its influence and of that culture's
present and future. They may well claim to find injustice in his
treatment. Still others may be as unsympathetic as White, while
rejecting the notion that this movement represents a dead end. For
example, René Girard shares much of the antagonism to structuralist and post-structuralist thinking, though he retains the hope of
working through it to an alternative that is anything but nihilistic.
Girard and Freedman, our remaining critics on this occasion, are
not so wide-ranging, both choosing to narrow-in on more limited
issues, though issues that are still central to some of the major
writers in our anthologies.

Girard concentrates his criticism on the structuralists' linguistic doctrine of difference. He sees this doctrine, in the work of
Lévi-Strauss, as being inflated into an absolute principle of both
theoretical method and metaphysical substance. The structuralist
attachment to such a principle leads Lévi-Strauss to elevate myth
(based on difference) and to reject ritual (based on undifferentiated immediacy). It is at this point that Girard levels his attack.
He sees Lévi-Strauss' distinction, invidious as it is to ritual, as
deriving from a dualism inherited from Bergson: with all methods
and all experience divided into the differentiated and the undifferentiated, Bergson's exclusive championing of the undifferentiated is answered by Lévi-Strauss' exclusive championing of the
differentiated. But Girard sees the two of them as clinging, with
equal metaphysical fervor, to a universal principle, whether that of
differentiation or that of undifferentiation, each rejecting the
other. Girard's concern is to deny polarity and the dualistic metaphysic that allows the inadequacy of either pole. Hence he argues
that not only ritual, but myth itself, reveals both undifferentiated
and differentiated elements in conjunction, claiming that only
Lévi-Strauss' unempirical devotion to a positivistic view of language

permits him to ignore the undifferentiated elements in myth and the differentiated elements in ritual. This argument opens out into his attack against the more general inadequacy to experience which he finds in the positivistic commitment to linguistic difference. (I am reminded of Adams' attack on the positivistic basis of structuralism and of White's treatment of post-structuralism as the farthest reach of the Western dualistic tradition.)

The central role of myth as Lévi-Strauss' agent of difference prompts Girard to use it as his weapon to turn structuralism against itself. He claims that Lévi-Strauss treats myth "not as 'differentiated' solely, as any text would be, but as differentiation displaying itself. Myth is not simply structured, it is structuralist." Thus myth is seen to be a paradigm of the symbolizing process as differential. In its commitment to the single process, "the all-purpose differentiating machine" endangers its own nature with the uniformity—the very sameness—of its application, whatever the objects on which it operates. Such *un*differentiation produces a self-contradiction. And it leads to the unprivileged equivalence among all its differentiated objects, appropriate to "the *société de consommation.*" This phrase recalls White's language about commodities and the indiscriminate reduction of all things to that status. For Girard it is the way in which difference undoes itself: "We cannot respect all differences equally without in the end respecting none."

But, unlike White, Girard is not ready to resign himself to the triumph of the fashion of differentiation turned into a metaphysical principle; instead, he belligerently tries to supersede it. For he feels he can renew the defense of religion and its source in ritual only by emphasizing those elements—mythical monsters, incest, sexual or hierarchical inversions—which disrupt the order that society's rational distinctions create, and *un*differentiate their communities. Perhaps the most basic of such undifferentiating rituals is the scapegoat. This arbitrarily chosen victim serves his community most ambiguously: through being uniquely differentiated from the others, he brings undifferentiated unity to the rest, and what was an arbitrary selection becomes necessary and indispensable through his function. In this manner the victim overcomes the arbitrary role of signifier to which a differential linguistics would relegate him. Such are the "rebellious phenomena" "that do not respond properly to the structuralist method." Only a stubborn positivistic allegiance, fearful of confronting human dis-

order with its irrational propensity to violence, would evade such
rebellious phenomena or demythify them away by subjecting their
irreducibly undifferential elements to "the all-purpose differentiating machine."

Once Girard has fastened onto victimage as the exemplary
ritual which exposes the inadequacy of structuralism, he can claim
that structuralism must respond to the threat posed to it by
turning ritual itself into its victim. Once again structuralism is
turned against itself: with Girard as our guide, we find Lévi-Strauss
enabled to define myth as he does (and, by negation, to define
ritual as he does) only by first enacting the ritual of expelling
ritual as *his* victim. We are to understand that "the arbitrariness
which characterizes the treatment of ritual ... duplicates exactly
the arbitrariness of the victim.... Ritual is expelled as the sole
and complete embodiment of the undifferentiated. This expulsion
is supposed to rid us once and for all of this 'evil mixture.' " What
could be more persuasive proof that victimage is the most basic of
symbols and the very source of our symbolizing power—whatever
structuralists may say—than the fact that structuralism itself, in
order to define myth as the source of its differential symbol-
making, must indulge in the ritual of victimage through the expulsion of ritual? Through this act the priority of symbolization is
granted to ritual, so that Lévi-Strauss is unwittingly proving Girard
rather than himself right. Structuralism thus engages in the ritual
that disproves its own first principle of universal difference: "Since
the undifferentiated is supposed to be entirely contained in ritual,
it is entirely expelled by the expulsion of ritual." So myth is
purified as an exclusively differential entity, except that the purifying act has undermined the ground on which it would stand.

Girard can now generalize his observation about Lévi-Strauss'
ritual act: "The horrified recoil from primitive ritual and religion
stems from the same impulse as religion itself, in the new circumstances brought about by this very religion." It is this claim which
enables him to resist the resignation I have sensed in White, who
perceives, in those who follow from structuralism, a final stage, an
ultimate revolutionary method, that undoes—while it consum-
mates—our culture's history. For Girard prefers to regard them as
too rigidly attached to just another privileged metaphysic—the
negative principle of difference—which post-structuralists like
Foucault and Deleuze institutionalize into an "epistemological
nihilism." Thus "Foucault correctly appraises the limitations of

this system [the structuralist] but he confuses them with the absolute limits of human language and of our power to know." Here, then, is a "particular scholar who seems primarily intent on a most scholarly burial of scholarship itself." These judgments echo somewhat those we have heard in White's essay, except that Girard claims to have found a way out of this dead end with his proposal of victimage as a ritual that is the true source of symbolization. Does he mean his essay itself to initiate such a move by its performing of the ritual expulsion of structuralism? If so, Girard himself has no obstacle in *his* system to prevent him from resorting to a ritual cure.

When he turns to the more exclusively literary sphere, Girard sees the same structuralist reduction at work, to the neglect (or should I say the expulsion?) of the less orderly stuff of human experience. Thus he calls for the approval and encouragement of works "which suggest some relationship, however indirect and tenuous, between human conflict and the principle of form, or structure." He finds hopeful examples in Derrida and Frye, and healthy earlier anticipations in Kenneth Burke. On the other hand, he sees Poulet's work on the circle as reflecting in literary criticism the unfortunate "process of anthropological neutralization," which ritualistically expels from his abstract mathematical analysis the disordering elements of human ritual, itself full of expulsive intent. What is needed instead is literary analysis that respects the "true mystery" of language: "The true mystery is that language is both the perfectly transparent milieu of empiricism and the prison-house of linguisticism."

As Girard orders his sequence of arguments, he leads us toward an infinite regress of ritual victimage. The expulsion we find in literature is expelled by an inhospitable theory of language, and this theory is in turn expelled by our theorist ritualistically defending the ritual of expulsion. Through this reflexive series we come to the primitive origin of expulsion, with the victim's ambiguous function as the root of all symbolization. Having returned us here, the theorist would have us begin the symbolizing chain again, this time less puritanically, less positivistically. This is, of course, to place an enormous burden on victimage since all symbolizing is to emerge from it and to repeat its essential pattern on increasingly sophisticated levels. Such a uniformity of pattern, continually susceptible of being reduced to its origins, is unhappily suggestive of the structuralist analysis from which it is supposedly exempt. Yet the residue of arbitrary violence persists, though rescued for order and community. But it cannot surrender its irrational nature even if the structuralist again tries to read it out of existence.

V

In our final essay, Ralph Freedman restricts his attention to a phenomenological interpretation of intentionality which he makes in the interest of reconciling modes of criticism often seen as disparate. He seeks a common intentionality which can fuse the poet as live person with the poem as his verbal object seen as such by living readers. Freedman, then, is one of White's "Normal" critics, firmly and imperturbably Normal. He tries to accommodate within his normalcy most of what our other critics have seen as threats to criticism. In this way he can, by means of his attachment to Valéry, become "Inflationary," and then can even expand to the "Generalizing" mood induced by his interest in Heidegger, still without letting go of that normalcy. Even with Heidegger he is never troubled by the temptation toward "Absurdism," though he does reject Barthes and what he sees as the structuralist tendency toward the dissolution of criticism. Only structuralism seems unaccommodatingly beyond the friendly and expansive confines of a Normal criticism that can embrace even the Heideggerian enlargement of consciousness to "conversation," while holding onto the sober commitment to the poem as verbal object.

Freedman presents four historical moments which portray paradigmatically the development of the fused intentionality he seeks. First, by way of the *dizain* of Scève, he shows how, through the Renaissance "emblem," the poet's feelings can be "neutralized and turned into literary objects while at the same time evoking a living mind." With no epistemological problem to haunt it, this poetic theory can use the emblem to lock the subjective into the object for permanent display. In Freedman's second moment, Diderot intrudes the temporality of the empirical self upon the lingering spatiality of the emblem. In a paradoxical awareness typical of the eighteenth century, he sees both the inner states of consciousness and a verbal object which alternately dissolves into time and retains its claim to spatial there-ness. Intentionality here is double and unreconciled. In the third moment, Freedman arrives, by way of Kant, at Valéry, whom he sees as completing the aesthetic prepared for by Kant. Kant resolves the dualism represented by Diderot, though he retains too much epistemological sophistication to *dis*solve it. Still, he frees himself to portray "an objective order . . . as an analogy to a structure of the mind," and thus frees modern criticism to develop theories of intentionality that can reconcile subject and object. Freedman sees Valéry as going farthest toward realizing these possibilities: the poet's self, moving through the "*état poétique*" to the "abstraction" that creates the object's world, retains that self in an utterly transformed verbal reality. "A relationship between the mind, the organization of the world, and the work of art exists, creating an order in which they all can cohere." But the order is firmly in the realm of the literary object. As Freedman puts it, to Valéry "the dance of the mind among things and the dance of things among minds, are caught in the verbal dance of poetry."

But there is yet a fourth moment, for Freedman is aware that, in Valéry's total commitment to the object, the delicacy of the Kantian balance may be unsettled. So he turns to the phenomenological tradition from Husserl to Heidegger in hopes that he can restore the centrality of consciousness while retaining the verbal object as its embodiment. He sees the notion of intentionality as providing for "the reciprocal relationship of subject and object *within* consciousness." Yet it must move outward as well. In Heidegger's essay on Hölderlin he finds the movement outward from the poem which does not lose it as poem. It is a movement from consciousness, via the poem, to other minds, to existence, and to historical existence. It occurs through the communal act of "conversation" in which "we" engage. But, for Freedman, so long as there is the need to return to the verbal notion of the "conversation," the poem is preserved: "In a poetic text we discern how a mind deals with its objects and confronts other minds, while remaining a single text in which all these relations are absorbed." Even the image in the Scève poem can be reexamined and used to reinforce this fourth paradigmatic moment. The mutuality between the lovers and the hair, in the language that constitutes that relationship, becomes an allegory of the Heideggerian conversation: in it "subject and object are therefore both separate and unified, for they exist in an identical realm of consciousness while reciprocally acting upon one another." Do we hear an echo of Girard in this claim to the coexistence of identity with difference?

Having come through our other essays, we should by now have noted that the price of this theoretical expansion has been what White referred to as the "generalizing" of criticism. The notion of "existence as a single conversation" collapses all of history into poetry in a way that certainly explodes the Normal critic's concern with actual poems. Freedman is himself aware that poetry is becoming synonymous with man's generally creative capacity as verbal creature, as the following description of Heidegger's position makes clear: "When man in general becomes a poet and language in general becomes poetry, a conductor from consciousness to Being by way of the existent may have been found. Poetry, then, is the language of history and existence. . . ." Earlier we saw that this neo-Kantian view of language, which would have it constituting all our reality, gave Adams reason to be wary, though not always—I then feared—wary enough. Nor does Freedman seem sufficiently concerned about the potential conflict between the "Inflationary" tendency of his version of Valéry and the "Generalizing" tendency of his version of Heidegger. Once expanded to conversation, can poetry ever again contract to the poem as he found it in Valéry?

The dominant theoretical mood in Freedman is one of reconciliation, perhaps more pleasant and appropriate for our final essay than the more embattled mood in the critics who preceded him. Would that we could blend our theories instead of having to choose ineluctably among them. But, as I have suggested, reconciliation has its price—usually the smoothing over of rough differences that turn opponents into allies. It is, Girard would remind us, a triumph of the undifferentiated over the differentiated— except that the analytical faculty of the theorist, in its search for order, overlooks differences at its peril. We may be worried about accepting the resolution Freedman finds in phenomenological criticism when we find that criticism to include—without distinction among them—a variety of theorists stretching "from Merleau-Ponty to Poulet, from Heidegger to Staiger." Poulet, in particular, hardly seems to warrant the designation as phenomenological in the way others may—especially the Poulet we have seen in discussions by our other critics. The inclusion of Poulet is the more troublesome when we see phenomenological criticism characterized as "hybrid formalism," in which "the uniqueness of the literary text is retained," so that, if "it seemed to solve the problem of the formalist isolation of the poem from life," it does so "without abandoning the inviolability of the poetic text." I fear that, as it applies to Poulet and to some of the others, this claim holds more hope and good will than truth. Freedman's commitment to Normal criticism, in its Inflationary mode, has persuaded him to broaden his fellowship to an inclusiveness in which theoretical incompatibilities may be overlooked. Only structuralist criticism, in which "the literary object is entirely eliminated," remains expelled—by Freedman as by Girard. He does not explore the fact that his reason—that "most structuralist theories ... reach ... toward that view of imagination which dissolves *all* art into life, and language, in general"—could be applied to some of those whom he termed phenomenological and whom he used to complete the merger between self and other, between self and text, which he sees as the achievement of the new intentionality. As perhaps a half-confession of the truth of what I have been suggesting, Freedman fittingly permits Valéry to return to have the last word about the *état poétique*.

VI

As I look back on what I have done, I feel that I must remind the reader of the relative safety of the scorecard-keeper. As he watches the play, he can point out flaws and still be lost in admiration. For he knows that he is not to be confused with the players and their greater risks, since he does not independently confront their tasks. Neither is his criticism subject to their overseeing. What I have found in these essays is a series of contrasts and parallels and overlappings too complex to mark them off briefly here in my conclusion. (I warned earlier of my impatience with scorecard shorthand.) But I did try to note some of them along the way. One generalization I must permit myself: there is among these critics no partisan—indeed there is little sympathy—for structuralism. I may have thought of these "directions for criticism" as dealing with "structuralism and its alternatives," but while there are plenty of alternatives, there is not much structuralism. It is, of course, frequently enough discussed (indeed it is treated prominently by all our critics), but only to be rejected. Either it is passed by on the way to post-structuralism (as in Said), or it is seen as too generalized a view of language which needs some supplementing (as in White or Freedman), or it is expelled altogether as a misleading theory (as in Adams or Girard). There is a general distrust of the projection of linguistic principles into a privileged metaphysic. Further, our authors share a concern about the positivistic element of reduction in structuralism, that which denies existence in its temporal fullness. The density of cultural data is not to be "signifier-ed" out of existence, signifying the decline of structuralism instead. And time is on their side. As for the alternatives to structuralism, those are what these pages have mainly been about.

An additional common feature of these essays should be noted. With the exception of Freedman, all of them at some point either have criticism turn on itself or discuss that criticism which turns on itself. They are, in other words, aware of the problematic of criticism, of criticism as a reflexive act that becomes its own object as well as—in the "Normal" sense—being a subject with another work as its object. Whatever their sympathies to this disposition in recent criticism (and they vary from participating in it to disdaining it), they recognize its revolutionary consequences, even (as in White or Girard) its tendency toward infinite regress. But most of all they are concerned with the loss of privilege suffered by the literary work in this reflexive dimension accorded criticism. And they must come to deal, as Said or White does, with the newly introduced competition between criticism and poetry—except that both arts have lost their discrete names and characters in the common democracy of *écriture*. About this problem all our critics concern themselves in ways that we have seen reflect their theoretical allegiances.

In thanking Professor Dembo for making this issue of *Contemporary Literature* available to us for tracking recent criticism in our several ways, I am really expressing my gratitude to him for recognizing criticism as a major form of contemporary literature, worthy of being studied as an object in its own right. This is to justify criticism as an "independent creation," as Said did; it is to justify works of criticism as appropriate replacements for the contemporary literary works normally treated in this journal as objects by a criticism functioning as what Said condescendingly called a secondary art, a subject serving its poetic object. But now I am using the ritual gesture of thanks as an occasion to press further that reflexive tendency in our criticism which, in its autotelic arrogance, threatens to do away with any object but itself. And I confess myself too much Hayden White's "Normal" critic not to counteract that tendency—to see it as a tendency to usurpation. Indeed, it is with some comfort that, as a "Normal" critic, I contemplate the return here, with the next issue, of properly literary objects of critical concern. I would say that it is an occurrence which should put all us critics in our place, were current criticism otherwise than it is, as we see it reflected in this issue.

Roads Taken and Not Taken in Contemporary Criticism

Edward W. Said

I

Even this handful of anthologies of modern literary theory and criticism[1] enables one to surmise that a very large quantity and variety of work is being done today. Yet these anthologies do not help one to estimate how much better (or worse), in general, literary criticism has become. Not only is it difficult to know with what to compare "modern" or "contemporary" criticism—with "classical" criticism? with "traditional" criticism? with the criticism of "a generation ago"?—it is next to impossible to get readers, much less professional critics, to agree about the purposes or effectiveness of criticism. Still more problematic is the distinction often made, but rarely explained, between critical theory and practical criticism, or between the theory *of* something and criticism of or about it. Surprisingly enough, sophisticated critical polemicists are more likely than one would imagine to be satisfied with crude national labels ("French" or "European" versus "English" or "American") in dealing with these issues and distinctions, and in letting them settle very large areas of intellectual discrimination. Names are often enough. "Frye" and "Leavis" stir up undignified passions; "Derrida" and "Leavis" might provoke

---

[1] For bibliographical details on the anthologies cited in this essay, see Krieger's introduction. Further references will cite the editor's name and the anthology page number only.

more rowdy emotions still. "Good"—in the sense of approved—criticism can thus be associated with Anglo-Saxon moral concern, evaluative assertion, a certain kind of attention to stylistic performance, an emphasis on "concrete" reading as opposed to "abstract" (and foreign) pseudo-philosophy or generality.

Stand on the other side of the net, and adjectives like "provincial," "untheoretical," "unproblematic," "unself-conscious" will be opening shots at the opponent; after that, one can hurl at him "structure," "semiological," "hermeneutical" and the more or less ultimate cross-court word "deconstruction." Any slightly more than casual reader of literary journals knows either repertoire, and probably yawns at them both—as much as he is also bored by any eclecticist who tries to use all the factional vocabularies to make a transcendental synthesis. But, in the manner of an impressionistic historian, one can say there *are* things about what goes on in contemporary criticism today that are typical, even representative of the mode. What assumptions would a clever anthologist make about his readers' interest in contemporary criticism, assuming that by "contemporary" he understood "criticism which one could not afford to ignore," or "criticism that seems, by its novelty, modishness, or sheer intellectual power, to make people believe that it is the representative, hence the vanguard, contemporary type"?

A question of this sort doesn't pretend to answer some of the basic problems faced by criticism. Neither, at the outset, does it get past the level of a useful exercise, by which one delineates the critical field in order to propose changes for it or reveal its shortcomings. If these anthologies serve any real function—aside from being convenient ways for the reader to get hold of fugitive essays—it is to let one think that they make up a consensus for today's critic, an immediate background he presumes to be accurate, from which he launches his own work, to which he responds, against which he defines himself, his allies, or his opponents. In accepting such a background the critic also presumes a background for the background, and without being too dodgy, he would say that these anthologies and what they represent aim to be different from previous anthologies and consensuses, which in turn were different from previous ones, etc. Critical change is much less sequential and abrupt than that, obviously enough. But let us grant a sense of change that these anthologies—dating roughly from the late sixties to the early seventies—incorporate and exploit. Whether such change is for the good of criticism or not is the issue to be dealt with only implicitly at first; later, in the second part of this essay, I would like to assess the change in terms of what this contemporary criticism cannot do, and in terms also of what it might be doing.

In a perfectly evident way, criticism today is more cosmopolitan than it has ever been since the first two decades of this century. (In order to make things easier, "criticism today"—and its cognates, "modern" or "contemporary criticism"—shall mean what it is that these anthologies stand for.) The Macksey-Donato collection (*The Languages of Criticism and the Sciences of Man*) most authoritatively records a seemingly lasting French intervention into American critical discourse, just as the conference of which it was the published proceedings was (in late 1966) the first important gathering of almost wholly foreign critics in the United States. The French intervention additionally caused doors and windows to be opened onto the rest of Europe, first onto Romance cantons and countries (Geneva and Italy, notably), then onto other areas like Germany, the Soviet Union, even the United States itself. And, indeed, the new cosmopolitanism revived interest in either old or native approaches—those of C. S. Peirce, philologists like Auerbach, Curtius, and Spitzer, as well as the Russian Formalists—previously known mainly to specialists.

A remarkable result for the practicing critic who wrote in English and who had an interest in theoretical issues was that English studies had its centrality eroded. Richard Poirier's well-known essay in Polletta's *Issues*,[2] already in 1970, spelled out the English-speaking critic's uneasiness with the position taken from Arnold to Leavis, that "our" moral center was to be found stretched out in the English classics. The touchstones were being transformed into *activity*, such as what Barthes called *l'activité structuraliste* and *écriture*,[3] or into a rather more generously conceived entity called modern literature. The latter is Lionel Trilling's phrase which, when he employed it first in 1961, resonated against Arnold in particular; that Arnold's best critic, as well as the critic whose work in the United States had most assuredly placed English

---

[2] Richard Poirier, "What Is English Studies, and If You Know What That Is, What Is English Literature?" in Polletta, pp. 557-71.

[3] See Roland Barthes, *Critical Essays*, trans. Richard Howard (Evanston: Northwestern Univ. Press, 1972), pp. 213-20; also his *Le Degré zéro de l'écriture suivi de Nouveaux essais critiques* (Paris: Seuil, 1972).

studies centrally on the literary agenda, spoke of a modern literature that included Diderot, Mann, Freud, Gide, and Kafka,[4] was a
significant announcement of how international and dialectical
English-speaking criticism had become.

Not only does it somehow seem pertinent to have had ses-
sions of the English Institute addressed in French about French
authors, but an intelligent young critic will now spend a lot of his
time reading and citing from Barthes, Derrida, Todorov, Genette,
and company. A new vocabulary—call it Anglo-French—disposes
terms like *découpage, décodage, bricolage*, with some assurance
that everyone will understand them. A fortunate few will quote
approvingly from Szondi, Benjamin, Adorno, Mayer, Enzensberger,
Raimondi, Eco, Lotman, and, of course, the ubiquitous Jakobson.
So it is not exceptionable that anthologies of the latest and best in
literary theory will draw most heavily on international, as opposed
to strictly local, work. From what had seemed to be the fierce
parochialism of New Criticism, for example, to the (sometimes)
abandoned cosmopolitanism of *this* New Criticism, it has mainly
been the isolated integrity of English studies—as a body of texts, as
a tradition, as an object, as a tone of voice, as a coherent,
well-defined discipline—that suffered in the change.

One could call the loss a loss of objectivity, in the sense of
objecthood. Notions of boundary, object-ness, limits, and with
them, the ideas of a national literature, a genre, a period, a
confined text, an author, seem to have weakened. The positivism
with which one could assert that romanticism is such and such, or
that the tradition is *those* works arranged in *that* order, has been
replaced with either a theory or a praxis of textual functions.
Barthes's critical theory, with its emphases on *écriture*, a defused
author (in his *Racine*), an omnicompetent text (in *S/Z*), a text as
sensation (in *Le Plaisir du texte*), fairly maps the shift from a kind
of objectivized historicism, with English or French studies at its
center, to a kind of international critical apparatus important for
its activity, not by any means for the literary material it may (or
may not) valorize. Curiously enough, a certain restraint has
operated on these anthologists who, while excerpting Barthes and
Todorov, have shied away from the most radical semioticians—
Kristeva, Sollers, Faye, and others—in the *Tel Quel* group. But that

---

[4] Lionel Trilling, "On the Teaching of Modern Literature," in Polletta, pp.
539-56.

is an omission, along with the avoidance of Ingarden and a still challenging Lukács, that I shall consider a little later.

On the one hand, there appears an international critical vocabulary aimed not at texts or traditions but at a condition of existence we may rightly call *textuality*; on the other hand, various counterorthodoxies arise to replace the orthodox notions of author, period, work, or genre. As is always the case with criticism, certain past authors seem suddenly important. Think of Dante or Donne and the New Critics; think of Hölderlin for Heidegger; think now of Artaud, Bataille, Saussure, Freud, Nietzsche for the latest new critics. Instead of these authors being touchstones they are employed rather as principles beyond which texts as texts cannot and need not go. To return to them, as Lacan returned to Freud, is to establish them in the role of a canon, whose legitimacy is maintained with loyal devotion. An unfortunate consequence for the assenting critic is that even if he does not use Arnold's image of venerable petrification as an equivalent for high value, he is no less susceptible to the dangers of received authority from canonical works and authors. A maddening new critical shorthand is to be observed. Instead of arguing a point, there tends often to be a lackluster reference to Nietzsche, or Freud, or Artaud, or Benjamin—as if the name alone carried just enough value to override any objection or to settle any quarrel. Most of the time the citation carries with it no discrimination that such a passage in such a work may be better or more useful than others, or less so in some unintentionally comic instances; the name and the reference are enough.

A new canon means also a new past or a new history, and less happily, a new parochialism. Any reader of modern French criticism will be astounded to realize that Kenneth Burke, in whose huge output many of the issues and methods currently engaging the French were first discussed,[5] is unknown. Is this the result of ignorance, or convenience, or deliberate ideological omission? Another example, for which the Europeans are not principally to blame, of course, is the slavish attitude to them by American critics. Yet what seems especially wasteful is the way one critic elaborates on or criticizes the work of a canonical critic—somebody

---

[5] Ignorance of Burke, and of Peirce, Dewey, Kroeber, Lowie, Sapir, Sullivan, and Mead is mentioned by Macksey in *The Languages of Criticism and the Sciences of Man*, p. 320.

like Barthes, or Derrida, for there is a living, producing canon,
too—and is never answered or even recognized by the canon.
Similarly, there is a pronounced tendency to avoid historical research, or its results, as something less interesting intrinsically than
theoretical speculation. Derrida's essays on Rousseau and Condillac,[6] to cite two very influential examples, have spawned a
whole array of imitations, all of them as historically and contextu-
ally thin as Derrida's were brilliant.

Inevitably we must ask, What then of the prevailing critical
discourse itself; or to be more exact and delimited, What does
critical discourse do? I shall speak here of a sort of majority *a
priori* belief that seems to direct critics' attention to one very
important aspect of the literary experience, namely *function*. In
most of the anthologized material we will find the critic talking
about what a text does, how it works, how it has been put
together in order to do certain things, how the text is a wholly
integrated and equilibrated system, and so forth. Much as it may
seem to be an impoverishing view of literature, this particular kind
of functionalism has had, on the whole, a salutary effect. It has
done away with empty rhetorical testimonials proclaiming a work's
greatness or humanistic worth. Moreover, it has made it possible
for critics to talk seriously and technically and precisely about the
text.

Here, there is some novelty to be remarked. Academic,
journalistic, or amateur criticism has usually been considered a
branch of belles-lettres; until the advent of American and English
New Criticism the job of a critic was an appreciation of the work,
which he was writing about as much for the "general" reader as
for other critics. Functionalist criticism makes the break between
the community of critics and the general public extremely sharp.
The assumption is that to write a literary work, or to write about
one, is a specialized function with no simple equivalent or cause in
everyday human experience. Therefore, critical vocabulary must,
and so does, emphasize the antinatural, and even antihuman, characteristics of verbal behavior in written language. And, since
genetic theses seem particularly suspect so far as literature is
concerned—writing cannot be reduced simply to a natural past, or

---

[6] Jacques Derrida, *De la Grammatologie* (Paris: Minuit, 1967) and his long
introduction *L'Archéologie du frivole* to Condillac's *Essai sur l'origine des
connaissances humaines* (Paris: Galilée, 1973).

to a natural urge, or to an empirically prior moment—the critic will go out of his way to find a technical language with no other possible use than to describe the text's functions.

An antecedent for this decision to employ a rigorous technical vocabulary based mainly upon linguistic terminology is found in I. A. Richards' criticism. He, of course, did not use linguistic terminology; but what distinguished hi.n, and Empson as well, from the American New Critics was his search for critical exactness without appeals either to the prestige of literature or of everyday experience. Precision in dealing with literature was gained for him in the use of words, and by what way can words be made precise except by a *science* of words, purified from inexactness, emotion, or sloppiness?

Richards' subsequent attention to Basic English, as well as his continued borrowings from ordinary language or utilitarian philosophy, and empirical psychology, set him apart from his contemporaries. What is additionally true of his work is also true of the critics we are discussing now—that the temptations of a rigorous technical critical vocabulary induce occasional lapses into a sort of scientism. Reading and writing become, at such moments, instances of regulated, systematized production, as if the human agencies involved were irrelevant. The closer the linguistic focus (i.e., in the criticism of Greimas or of Lotman, neither of whom has been anthologized), the more formal the approach; and the more scientistic the functionalism. And the more limited the defined functions.

Definitions, more often than not, point the reader back towards the method, since one aim of functionalism is to perfect the instrument of analysis as much as one's understanding of a text's workings. Thus while a really intelligent critic like Barthes will have the good taste to know the qualitative difference between Ian Fleming and Balzac, what he actually says is that the latter *works* better (is more responsive to a full-scale semiological reading by Barthes) than the former. This is almost as much as saying that you could write a good story if you knew the rules of composition, which obviously cannot guarantee any such result. For practical purposes, however, the constant peril of a functionalist bias is in giving the reader uniform, unvarying claustrophobia. Since the relationship between the work and the critic is a self-sealing and self-perpetuating one, since the specialized character of the relation is exclusive and rigidly systematic, a reader can expect

only to receive knowledge of a sort already confirmed and enclosed by the initial definitions. One experiences the text making
the critic work, and he in turn shows the text at work: the
product of these interchanges is simply that they have taken place.
Critical ingenuity is pretty much confined to transposing the
work—any work—into an instance of the method.

It is the potential monotony of this (or of any hermeticism
for that matter), not its apparent solipsism, that I find objection-
able. Most great critics are methodical; this perhaps means only
that they are able to articulate and rationalize their intuitive
awareness of literature. But it also means that they are not afraid
of making their methods and their own writing independently
interesting and intellectually consistent, over and above a work or
an occasion. For the lesser critic such challenges are rare. He will
use the work in order to make it work, which it always will. His
method will demonstrate its effectiveness, which it will always
possess. And on and on, without any sense of the drama underlying method, or of its fundamental ground in intellectual life.

The great virtue of Derrida's essay, "Structure, Sign, and Play
in the Discourse of the Human Sciences," is that method is shown
turning upon itself at the very moment of its greatest victories, in
order to achieve a still more novel, more differentiated lucidity.
Derrida goes on to say that "the risk of sterility and of sterili-
zation has always been the price of lucidity,"[7] and hints with
appropriate courage that he is willing to pay the price. But these
are partial statements made with a full realization that contemporary methodology occurs at a particular moment in human self-
consciousness, not randomly because a method was thought of and
then employed at will. Such essays as Derrida's are occasionally to
be found in the anthologies: their value is to make explicit a sense
of what I called the drama of method and its underlying roots in
intellectual vitality. Thereafter we are better enabled to recognize
that contemporary critical discourse is fundamentally antidynastic
in its attitudes—to the work, to the critic, to knowledge, to reality.
Orphaned by the radical Freudian, Saussurian, and Nietzschean
critique of origins, traditions, and knowledge itself, contemporary
criticism achieved its methodological independence by forfeiting an
active situation in the world. It has no faith in traditional con-

---

7 Jacques Derrida, "Structure, Sign, and Play in the Discourse of the
Human Sciences," in Macksey and Donato, p. 271.

tinuities (nation, biography, period); rather it improvises, in acts of an often inspired *bricolage*, order out of extreme discontinuity. Its culture is a negative one of absence, anti-representation, and (as Blackmur used to put it repeatedly) ignorance.

Learned or gifted ignorance is no mean thing, however. All of the major critics now writing make themselves over into critical instruments, as if from scratch; for their presumptive ignorance makes possible the finding out of important truth about, and important methods for, the study of literature. Consider a constellation of critics that might include Auerbach, Spitzer, Blackmur, Barthes, Genette, and Benjamin; their careers span almost a century, but a good deal of overlap occurs between them. All are comprised within the scope of our anthologies. Each of them, to begin with, is a reader whose learning is *for* the text, and whose method is *from* the text. Having said that, one would immediately remark that the divergences between them are very wide because of the ways each uses to doctor his ignorance. Yet none cares much for tidy distinctions between bloodless theory and practice, or between literary criticism and philology, philosophy, linguistics, psychology, sociology. Such as it is, their common method is incorporative; it converts what seems to be alien material, or in some cases quixotic and trivial material, into pertinent dimensions of the text.

Some of these dimensions appear perforce eccentric, even determinedly so. But this will-to-eccentricity, I think, is a major project of contemporary critical discourse, Northrop Frye's included. For the critic, texts are texts not as symbols of something else, but as *displacements* (Frye's vocabulary is useful here) of other things; texts are deviations from, exaggerations and negations of, human presence. They are at times phenomena of excess and of rupture. Style does not represent an author, any more than he *is* his biography. Instead the facts of style exist together in an affiliative, rather than a filiative, relation to a text, which itself is part of an affiliative structure of eccentric elements. All of this is a much-noted consequence of subjectivity's weakened position with regard to a text. No longer is it commonly held that Taine's data (*race, moment, milieu*) both exhaust and define the writer as the producer of his text; even as staunch a defender of fertile authorial consciousness as Poulet, accepts before anything else the eccentricity, contingency, and instability of self, its mutability and powerlessness before the text. "Reading, then, is the act in which

the subjective principle which I call *I*, is modified in such a way
that I no longer have the right, strictly speaking, to consider it as
my *I*."[8]

What makes such statements methodologically valid, as
opposed to being testimonials of an overly effusive sympathy
between critic and text, is that the critic's proper identity, his
working point of departure, is neither an empirical self (the same
self that eats, goes shopping, breathes, dies) nor a sort of official
persona. Instead, the critical identity, which one might as well also
call the critic's *author*itative, *author*izing method of dealing with
texts, is built upon a linguistic base, not a psychological, social, or
historical one. In effect, this means that language is considered as a
community of language-users, not merely as a means of communication. Such a community is intersubjective of course, but it has
rules or codes that give it order, coherence, intelligibility. The
critical method—whether Auerbach's, Spitzer's, Blackmur's,
Barthes's, Poulet's, or almost any one of the others—is effective
because as far as it is concerned, every aspect of language is
significant. And the production of significance is precisely the
principal capability of language. What concerns the critic is how
language signifies, what it signifies, and in what form.

A vast range of possibilities immediately opens out: are these
linguistic significations intentional? are they all equal? is one signification more determined historically or sociologically than
another? how do they influence each other?—the list of options for
critical attention can be extended to include every critical act. For
the critic is, of course, an intelligent reader first of all, but his role
after that is nothing if not an active and dialectical one. For it is
his work—his existence, his role—that makes, indeed determines,
significance as a subject for study and analysis. Thus the history of
literary criticism, as Hazard Adams' fine anthology amply demon-
strates,[9] is the history of critical mediations, which is another way
of saying that it is a history of critics gaining identity by endowing
certain linguistic objects with significance for the critic, and after
that, for other critics and readers. The critical identity is the
presentational device for certain, formally determined matters in

8 Georges Poulet, "Phenomenology of Reading," in Polletta, p. 107. The
essay was first contained in *The Languages of Criticism and the Sciences of Man*.

9 Hazard Adams, ed., *Critical Theory Since Plato* (New York: Harcourt
Brace Jovanovich, 1971).

language. To study the history of criticism is in reality to understand the history of literature critically; such a history is, no less than the history of biology described by François Jacob, "de rechercher comment les objets sont devenus accessibles à l'analyse, permettant ainsi à de nouveaux domaines de se constituer en sciences."[10]

II

The functionalist attitude in critical discourse (as I discussed it above) has some fairly unfortunate limitations, however. A functionalist attitude pays too much attention to the text's formal operations, but far too little to what I prefer to call its *materiality*. In other words, the range assumed for the text's operations tends to be either wholly internal or wholly rhetorical, with the critic himself serving as a sort of one-man *Rezeptionsgeschichte*. On the one hand, the text is imagined as working alone within itself, as containing a privileged, or, if not privileged, then unexamined and *a priori*, principle of internal coherence; on the other hand, the text is considered as in itself a sufficient cause for certain very precise effects it has on a (presumed) ideal reader. In both cases, therefore, the text does not remain but is metamorphosed into (*pace* Stanley Fish) a self-consuming artifact. A perhaps unforeseen consequence is that the text becomes idealized, essentialized, instead of remaining as the very special kind of cultural object which it really is, with a causation, persistence, durability, and social presence quite its own.

Some notable omissions from the anthologies indicate this prevailing idealist and antimaterialistic bias. Michel Foucault is nowhere to be found, and neither is any of the current *Tel Quel* group. Auerbach and Spitzer—whose predominantly philological scholarship is mainly concerned not with "reading" but with describing the modes of *persistence* of texts—are misrepresented completely; an untutored reader will assume (if he does not read the two or three essays *about* Spitzer and Auerbach) that they were rather old-fashioned versions of Brooks or Warren. Lukács stands out as a dull polemicist for "realism" since the company he keeps, anthologically speaking, actually extols artistic isolation and

---

[10]François Jacob, *La Logique du vivant: Une histoire de l'hérédité* (Paris: Gallimard, 1970), p. 19.

the value of aesthetic rarefication. The extracts from his work are
uniformly the same in critical anthologies generally, and uniformly
uninteresting as a result, since they are chosen simply, and unin-
terestingly, to prove his Marxism; the choice of such a Lukács
owes nearly everything to the cold war. [11]

Even in their efforts to give some idea of how resourceful the
functionalists are about *style* as a major instrument of the text's
activity, the anthologies do not excerpt work by Michael Rif-
faterre, M.A.K. Halliday, or other vigorous stylisticians. Moreover,
such sophisticated historical criticism as the anthologies present
cannot compare in its isolation from sociocultural history with
straight history-of-ideas writing, which often fills the pages of the
scholarly journals. This insensitivity to history spoils the very
matter being anthologized; history is therefore irrelevant. Gras's
anthology of modern "European Literary Theory" is grotesquely
portrayed without Ingarden, the Sartre of *What Is Literature?* and
The Critique of Dialectical Reason, or the Heidegger of *Being and
Time*.

These complaints are part of a peculiar disorder in modern
criticism itself. Criticism has given very little notice to its history
as a discipline—and any critic had better claim that criticism is a
discipline if it is not to be an intellectual equivalent only of wine
tasting. This essay is a perfect example of that disorder, since the
hedges with which I surrounded my opening definitions of
"modern criticism" make a great deal of what follows them appear
impressionistic at best. One of the signs of modern criticism—and
this is not impressionism—is a willingness to write criticism of
other critics. But it is comparatively rare to find critics undertaking
critical *histories* of criticism itself. True, there are encyclopedic
efforts like those of René Wellek, but we must ask why the
preference in critical history is always for the encyclopedia (hand-
book, anthology, casebook, etc.) and rarely, if ever, for the *critical*
critical history. Such a history would undoubtedly entail consideration of social and political impingements on criticism; it would also
require attention to the question of when criticism is a discipline
and when not. In short, critical attention to criticism viewed as an

---

11 The other Lukács, by no means inconsistent with the assertively Marxist
Lukács, is to be found in *Soul and Forms, The Theory of the Novel, Die
Eigenart das Ästhetischen*, and variously in his *Schriften zur Ideologie* and
Literatursoziologie.

intellectual phenomenon in a historical, social setting is resisted in ways exactly congruent with those I have listed for functionalist attitudes, which view the text as something immaterial. Criticism is considered as what critics do, irrespective of their archival or worldly circumstances. To produce criticism is to do what has always been done, with no change or past to speak of.

For the anthologist, particularly if he is concerned with the modern, an anthologized choice (or exclusion) is often dictated by the sheer unintelligibility of a potential choice, since excerpts are even harder to understand than a whole book. Packageability is more relevant than historical, or even aesthetic, accuracy. But that is not always the case. What we will detect, then, is a conscious avoidance of criticism whose focus is the text as something other, as something historically and materially more, than a critical occasion. But what do I mean by "material" in this case? I mean the ways, for example, in which the text is a monument, a cultural object sought after, fought over, possessed, rejected, or achieved in time. Moreover, the text's materiality includes the range of its authority. Why does a text enjoy currency at one time, recurrency at others, oblivion at others? [12] By the same token, an author's *fama*, his reputation, his status, is by no means a constant thing; is an account of this inconstancy, or at least, this inconsistency, not within the critic's job of work? It is, I believe, the more so now that the possibilities of archeological historical research have been so extended and refined by Foucault.

Foucault's method is to study the text as part of an archive, which is composed of discourses, which are composed of statements. In short, he deals with texts as part of a system of cultural diffusion, rigidly controlled, tightly organized, difficult to penetrate: he argues that everything stated in a field like literary discourse, for example, or medical discourse, is produced only with the most selective method, with very little regard for individual genius. [13] Each statement is therefore a material effort to incorporate a particular piece of reality as selectively as possible.

---

[12] For analyses of these problems see my "An Ethics of Language," *Diacritics*, 4, No. 2 (Summer 1974), 28-35; *Beginnings: Intention and Method* (New York: Basic Books, 1975), pp. 191-275; "The Text, the World, the Critic," *Bulletin of the Midwest Modern Language Association*, 8, No. 2 (Fall 1975), 1-23.

[13] See Michel Foucault, *The Archaeology of Knowledge*, trans. A. M. Sheridan Smith (New York: Pantheon, 1972), pp. 79-131.

But there are other ways of dealing with the materiality of
texts, and these too are scanted by the anthologies. The opposite of incorporation as discussed by Foucault, no less material,
is the theme of literary influence as recently theorized
(and troped) by W. J. Bate and Harold Bloom. [14] Here, too, context is of the essence, since their assumption is that every writer,
but especially the romantic post-Miltonic writer, is almost bodily
aware of his predecessors as occupying the poetic space he now
wishes to fill with his poetry. The intertextual struggle for the
poet, according to Bloom, is no charming tea party, but a fierce
battle whose all-pervading jostle spills over into, and becomes the
topic of, the new, late-coming poet's verse. The text's materiality
here is what the poetry *is*, and whether it can be a poetic text or
not is something never taken for granted by the poet. Each line, in
short, is an achievement, a space snatched out of the predecessor's
clutches, filled by the poet with his words, which in time will
have to be fought over by a successor. The family romance of
poetry as Bloom and Bate portray it breeds a defensive poetry, a
child of limitation and defensive anxiety.

What Foucault, Bloom, and Bate have in common is that their
work is about, and indeed is, the text's situation in the world;
Foucault's, of course, is the world of culture, Bloom's and Bate's
the world of art. One almost finds oneself saying that criticism
always ought to be in the world, and that any world will do. But
that is a sloppy notion, which I have tried elsewhere to hone a
bit. [15] Yet compared not only with Foucault, Bate, and Bloom, but
with the unreasonably ignored work of Raymond Schwab, [16] contemporary critical discourse is worldless, in a frequently numbing
way. Considering that much of the truly valuable work in literary
theory and scholarship being done now in America is about romanticism (and note, by the way, that the anthologies before us are
remarkably stingy on poetics or the various theories of poetic
performance), there seems to be no good reason for keeping
Schwab out. His thesis in *La Renaissance orientale* is a simple one:

---

14 See W. J. Bate, *The Burden of the Past and the English Poet* (Cambridge: Harvard Univ. Press, 1970); and Harold Bloom, *The Anxiety of Influence: A Theory of Poetry* (New York: Oxford Univ. Press, 1973), as well as his
A Map of Misreading (New York: Oxford Univ. Press, 1975).

15 See my "The Text, the World, the Critic," pp. 18-22.

16 In particular Schwab's *La Renaissance orientale* (Paris: Payot, 1950), but
also his *Vie d'Anquetil-Duperron* (Paris: Ernest Leroux, 1934).

that romanticism cannot be understood unless some account is taken of the great textual and linguistic discoveries made about the Orient during the late eighteenth and early nineteenth centuries. To be convincing, such a thesis needs to be buttressed with a tremendous amount of detail drawn from history, sociology, literature, Orientalism itself, philosophy, and linguistics. Schwab has the detail, but what is more to the point for a critical theorist, he can organize it superbly, not according to a reductive linear scheme, but in terms of a subtle analysis of the process of gradual, then increasingly rapid, acculturation of the Orient by European society and culture.

Schwab's point is that texts are frequently the result of an encounter between familiar and novel ideas; yet such an encounter is eminently circumstantial and material, as when Anquetil-Duperron risks his life trying to get hold of the Zend-Avesta texts in Surat, texts which he then translates for the benefit of European culture at large. The innumerable and sometimes minute facts of such encounters are destined by Schwab to support his view of the change in European cultural institutions as a result of their reception of the Orient. Individual texts are seen from a perspective that is also able to pull in the salon, the museum, the laboratory, the learned academies, and even bureaucratic and governmental organizations.

I cite Schwab, Foucault, Bate, and Bloom as exemplifying a possible trend for criticism to be taken seriously only if literature is going to be studied in a more situated, circumstantial—but no less theoretically self-conscious—way. Of course, there is no point in my further qualifying "situated" and "circumstantial" since it should be obvious that I mean "worldly" and "historical": for literature is produced in time and in society by human beings, who are themselves agents of, as well as somewhat independent actors within, their actual history. For some reason contemporary vanguard criticism has assumed that the relations between texts, and between texts and society, are taken care of by the superstructure or by something called "traditional" scholarship. That assumption is not warranted, if one means by the relation between texts and society anything like the complexity assigned to it by Benjamin (the student of Baudelaire), the Goldmann of *Le Dieu caché*, or Lukács. So-called traditional scholarship has rarely possessed the methodological rigor and vision of such critics. But the critics of influence have at least the great merit of believing that literature is

produced *because* of other poets and texts, *in* their company, not
despite them. Schwab and Foucault, the former in actual practice,
the latter in extremely powerful theory, have gone very far in
determining the social (and external) constraints upon production,
as well as the discursive and cultural (that is, internal) systems that
provoke and assimilate literary production.

To approve and admire such historically generous critics is by
no means to overlook problems in their theory and practice. From
the viewpoint of learning, however, nothing they say has that
airless and technically lucid finality characterizing a structural *crite-
fact*, to coin a neologism for what is in fact only an analytical
neologism; but in my opinion Schwab's and Foucault's work places
too great a premium upon dramatic change. To a different degree,
the same is no less true of Bate and Bloom. Literary history has
been regarded by them all as a more or less steady drama, with
one great age succeeded riotously by another. History in such a
view becomes at bottom "linear succession" even though what-
succeeds-what is described in very complex nonlinear detail. Only
recently Foucault has tried rather programmatically to understand
textual history in terms of those comparative stabilities (borrowing
from Braudel) he called "the slow movements of material civilization." [17] Perhaps this refocusing on how texts maintain, instead
of always changing, history is a return to Foucault's early interest
in Raymond Roussel (e.g., "Les machineries de Roussel ne fabri-
quent pas de l'être; elles maintiennent les choses dans l'être"). [18]

What is it that maintains texts inside reality? What keeps
some of them current, while others disappear? How does an
author imagine for himself the "archive" of his time, into
which he proposes to put his text? What are the centers of
diffusion by which texts circulate? For example, what equivalents
in early nineteenth-century English culture are there for the French
academies and the literary-scientific Parisian *salons* as agents of
cultural dispersion and organization? Goldmann's theory of
homologous structures, while it anticipates some of these questions,
does not go far enough in beginning to answer them. Moreover, we
need to understand with precision what role critical scholarship
plays and has played in the production of "literary" works, a
question raised seriously by both Wilde and Nietzsche. For

---

17 Foucault, *The Archaeology of Knowledge*, p. 3.
18 Michel Foucault, *Raymond Roussel* (Paris: Gallimard, 1963), p. 96.

example, how are the great philological discoveries contemporary with the European Romantic Movement influential in poetry, remembering that Coleridge, the Schlegels, Hölderlin, Chateaubriand and others were writers with a deep interest in those discoveries? What method do we have for methodically assimilating such verbal institutions in a given social era as narrative, philology, history? In what way are etymology in philology, and plot succession in the novel related? To call them all "textual phenomena" is hardly a satisfying answer, but so far this is all the answer we get. Of what moment to literary history are the rift in relations among language and philosophy and religion, which had been aligned together at the end of the eighteenth century, and the new rapprochement between language and natural science (comparative anatomy in particular) by the first third of the nineteenth century? Locke and Sterne; Balzac and Cuvier or Geoffroy Saint-Hilaire. Here there is no question of derived ideas but of their inherent currency, or recurrency if you prefer.

Any attention to these and similar questions must draw the critic very far into the rationale of his work. One of the unfortunate losses in contemporary critical discourse is that sense critics once had of their work as an intellectual adventure. An earlier tradition, which lasted until the middle of the eighteenth century, was the scholar's (or critic's) consideration of his life as having exemplary value; scholarly biography was a recognized genre. In both instances what the critic did, how he went from work to work, how he formulated the projects he undertook, were treated as meaningful parts of the methodological experience, not simply as anecdotal tidbits.

I draw notice to these historical aspects of critical practice in order to approve their value for the future of critical discourse. Pedagogically, there is every good reason for regarding the choice of a subject and its formulation as being not only the beginning of a critical project, but also the critical project itself. If, therefore, we would have accounts by critics of what led them to a given project, why and how they fashioned the project, how they undertook its completion and in what context, we would have opportunities for future study of a very important sort. Not only would it be possible to understand once and for all that criticism creates its subject matter—there are no problems lying about to be dealt with—but also young critics would understand criticism to be an activity whose main purposes are the enablement of learning and

the multiplication of critical discourse, from restriction to comparative freedom. If critics today often feel that they are paralyzed
by the sheer difficulty of finding a subject about which to write, it
is because they have not realized the part of independent creation
in criticism.

For in a very deep way, critical discourse is still ensnared by a
simplistic opposition between originality and repetition, in which
all literary texts worth studying are given the former classification,
the latter being logically confined mainly to criticism and to what
isn't worth studying. I believe such schema to be hopelessly para-
lyzing. They mistake the regularity of most literary production for
originality, while insisting that the relation between "literature"
and criticism is one of original to secondary; moreover, they
overlook, in both traditional and modern literature, the profoundly
important constitutive use of repetition—as motif, device, epistemology, and ontology. [19] Perhaps it is not until the nineteenth
century that such a view of repetition becomes explicit (in Kier-
kegaard, Marx, Nietzsche, for instance), though Curtius and Auerbach have taught us that that is not really the case. From its
earliest beginnings narrative fiction, to take a further example, has
been built around the tantalizing figure of the family, in which its
recurring circumstantial perpetuity is tampered with (unsuccessfully) by the upstart "original" hero. Why this modal constancy if
not to preserve, maintain, repeat, the form of fiction within the
"slow movements of material civilization"?

As for the relationships in value between originality and ideas
of novelty, of primacy, or of "the first"—this is a crucial matter.
All critics take for granted that there is some connection between
a great work and (on some level at least) its priority. Bloom's
theory of influence is built around this notion, that a great work
has power because it is, or was, first, that it came before and
preempted others. Now such ideas also carry with them an extremely crude understanding of what it means to be first, or to
have come first. The necessity of such biological crudeness—it is
biological, since "first" means "father" and "second" means
"son"—for Bloom is unquestioned; he uses it, and it is by no
means incidental to his poetics of misreading.

---

[19] See my "On Originality," in *Uses of Literature*, ed. Monroe Engel,
Harvard Studies in English, No. 4 (Cambridge: Harvard Univ. Press, 1973),
49-65.

But for other critics priority is associated rather lackadaisi-
cally with novelty, with coming or happening first, with simple
precedence, as if history were like a series of children being born
one after the other from past to present ad infinitum. An irreducibly serial, filiative conception of sociohistorical time such as
this, totally obscures the very interesting problem of emergence, in
which cultural phenomena are not simply ascribed priority or a
miraculous "birth," but rather treated as a "family of ideas"
emerging "permanently in discourse." [20] Cultural events are not
best understood as if they were human beings born on a certain
day; the past is not a set of such births, and time does not move
like a clock, in discrete succession. The history of science has
learnt to deal with the emergence problem, why not literary
theory? What are the limits to employing the human life cycle as a
model of literary history? How really useful is a critical approach
based on anthropomorphic units of originality like "work,"
"author," "generation," and so forth? What vocabulary can we
employ that deals with human agency as well as the impersonal
repeating discourse of literary structure?

These are difficult questions to answer, but they are indispensable ones to the development of a critical discourse which will be
intellectually serious and socially responsive in the largest humane
sense. Only if the development occurs will it be possible dialecti-
cally to assess the genuine force, in literary history and institutions, of threats to coherence or order. There is no way to grasp
these threats so long as cultural history is viewed as a lazy series of
births and deaths. If culture is maintained materially then it cannot
be dependent on events but on institutions constructed by men,
these institutions also having an independent history of their own.

The dialectical opposite of the repeating, maintaining material
civilization to which I have been referring is an allied set of
forces—Blackmur called them collectively the Moha [21] —whose
presence in human life disturbs, wastes, troubles the numenal
coercion of culture. One of the signal achievements of psycho-
analytic criticism has been the attempt to deal with the Moha. Yet,

[20] Ian Hacking, *The Emergence of Probability: A Philosophical Study of
Early Ideas About Probability, Induction and Statistical Inference* (London:
Cambridge Univ. Press, 1975), p. 17.
[21] R. P. Blackmur, *The Lion and the Honeycomb: Essays in Solicitude and
Critique* (New York: Harcourt, Brace and World, 1955), pp. 289-309.

too often, symptology, or the mere willingness to consider this force as culturally deviant (whereafter it is confined to the neurotic weaknesses of the artist), has resulted. Recently the French attention both to Nietzsche and Freud has remedied the situation, but we need a more situated account of the Moha *getting in* to literature. This is a current of critical analysis begun effectively by Georges Bataille in 1933 with "La Notion de dépense." [22] To date, the challenge has not been taken up except in Morse Peckham's *Man's Rage for Chaos* and in Richard Poirier's *The Performing Self.* [23]

The interplay of order and disorder frames the essentially dispersed, diffused, disseminated sense of the literary text. Within that frame, however, there is an entire order of genetic questions, fearfully neglected since the 1944-45 Wimsatt-Beardsley attack on intention, an attack continued in Wimsatt's forceful "Genesis: A Fallacy Revisited," reprinted by Polletta. [24] Certainly one must feel that the irreducible dualities—subjective/objective, inside/outside, author/poem, and so on—held on to by Wimsatt and others extort too high a cost in understanding and discrimination. Furthermore, there is a large body of modern literature beseeching the reader to make intentional leaps into the author's psyche and into his own (see Trilling's essay, "On the Teaching of Modern Literature" or Blackmur's four essays, *Anni Mirabiles*). [25] Strict boundaries between self and object, or ego and world, encourage a useful, yet preliminary, pedagogical discipline; nevertheless they are not about, and they do not describe anything more than, an analytic reality. Thus Goldmann writes:

Every manifestation [of intellectual and artistic phenomena] is the work of its individual author and expresses his thought and his way of feeling, but these ways of thinking and feeling are not independent entities with respect to the actions and behaviour of other men. They exist and may be understood only

---

22 "La Notion de dépense," in *La Part maudite* (Paris: Minuit, 1967).

23 Peckham, *Man's Rage for Chaos: Biology, Behavior and the Arts* (Philadelphia: Chilton Books, 1965); Poirier, *The Performing Self* (New York: Oxford Univ. Press, 1971).

24 W. K. Wimsatt, "Genesis: A Fallacy Revisited," in Polletta, pp. 255-76.

25 See R. P. Blackmur, *Anni Mirabiles 1921-1925: Reason in the Madness of Letters*, in *A Primer of Ignorance*, ed. Joseph Frank (New York: Harcourt, Brace and World, 1967), pp. 3-80.

in terms of their inter-subjective relations which give them their whole tenor and richness.... [26]

If we accept this argument, then our responsibility is to venture beyond the rudimentary demarcations.

I see no particular use in constantly insisting that a poem is a solitary object, for it clearly is not. Each poem or poet is involuntarily the expression of collectivities; what becomes an interesting theoretical problem for criticism is to determine how, or when, or where, the poet or his poem can be said to be a voluntary (i.e., personal and/or intentional) expression of difference and/or community. Here genesis is not a simple empirical idea like birthdate, which has no special genetic power of explanation, but a conceptual test of critical interpretation. To admit that we now have only *some* genetic theses about literary production is quite another thing from saying categorically that there can never be a satisfactory genetic thesis. (See my comments above on the "emergence" problem.) A Luddite approach to what after all is in the critic's possession as a sentient rational historical being—the capacity to make genetic hypotheses—is a violent denial of some portion of his humanity. For genetic hypotheses, such as how or why such and such a work came to be written, are not one-way referrals of "a" work back to biography, or society, or whatever, just as iconic or textual studies need not always, and by definition, exclude the historical context surrounding the text. A genetic hypothesis admits the notion of human agency into the work—not a very daring idea in itself. But the obligation to rational interpretation along these lines goes further to include as part of the dialectic the critic's own shaping awareness of what he is doing. This awareness obviously increases and is refined in the very act of making a critical method.

Perhaps one way of imagining the critical issue of aesthetic genesis is to view the text as a dynamic field, rather than as a static block, of words. This field has a certain range of reference, a system of tentacles, partly potential, partly actual—to the author, to the reader, to a historical situation, to other texts, to the past and present. In one sense no text is finished, since its potential range is always being examined, hence extended, by every addi-

---

[26] Lucien Goldmann, *The Human Sciences and Philosophy*, trans. Hayden White and Robert Anchor (London: Jonathan Cape, 1969), p. 128.

tional reader. Now the critic's task is obviously first to understand (in this case understanding is an imaginative act) how the text *was* and *is* made. No details, and their provenance, are too trivial, provided one's study is directed carefully towards the text as a vital aesthetic and cultural whole. The critic therefore mimes, or repeats, the text in its extension from beginning to whole, not unlike Pierre Ménard. Or like Proust in his pastiches of Flaubert, Balzac, Renan, and the Goncourt brothers. In making over the authors he imitated, Proust set himself the aim of producing them from the opening to conclusion of a passage. Only by re-producing can we know what was produced and what the meaning of verbal production is for a human being: this is the quintessential Vichian maxim. And it is no less valid for the literary critic for whom the genesis of a human work is as relevantly interesting as its being, since both are infrangibly connected.

I need add only one more thing to these last remarks. The prevailing ideology of even advanced literary criticism today is pronouncedly ethnocentric and seems indifferent to everything but the politico-social status quo. I shall not advocate any specific program to alter this, but will restrict myself to some observations and a final question or two. Every great age of literature and criticism has had organic ties with a dominant value system of some sort. All critics of the past have held fairly explicit views of man, his destiny, his goods, goals, nature. In other words, literary criticism has always contained some sense of its place in the process of human history. For reasons I cannot quite articulate, this is not true of contemporary critical discourse. In most instances it is disturbingly quietistic. Moreover, one gets no inkling from it that there are other literatures and languages than those of the Atlantic-European community, nor that vast segments of human society express other modes of aesthetic experience than the Occidental. That all this should be taking place as well in a world of exacerbated political and economic crisis increases one's wonderment at the ideological and evaluational silence of criticism today. What is the meaning of such silence? Need such silence be?

Contemporary Ideas
of Literature:
Terrible Beauty
or Rough Beast?

Hazard Adams

Anthologies of things "modern" or "contemporary" have short lives. As soon as they appear they are out of date. This is most obvious with books produced on the crest of new movements or designed to introduce relatively unfamiliar material. The books under discussion all ride a crest, with the exception of *In Search of Literary Theory*, which has an air of familiarity.[1] This crest is the movement into the American ken of certain modern continental modes of criticism and that mixture of them known in France as the *nouvelle critique*. It is a difficult task for the anthologists to make the necessary introductions when the movements themselves are still subject to dynamic revision and inner strife and at a point when positions are still being worked out or asserted, rather than analyzed. Though Saussure's linguistics, certain phenomenological approaches, and the work of prominent figures like Jakobson and Bachelard have been around for a long time, there is no history of continental critical developments. There has been much debate and invective, but the sort of analysis that Murray Krieger so ably

---

[1] *In Search of Literary Theory* contains essays by M. H. Abrams, E. D. Hirsch, Jr., Northrop Frye, Geoffrey Hartman, Paul de Man, and the editor, Morton W. Bloomfield. For bibliographical details on the anthologies cited in this essay, see Krieger's introduction. Further references will cite the editor's name and the anthology page number only.

performed for the American New Criticism as early as 1956[2] is only now beginning to appear, the most formidable example being Jonathan Culler's *Structuralist Poetics*.[3] As a result there has not yet been a satisfactory sifting down in these or any other volumes, and there has been some difficulty in finding quite the representative texts. Barthes's "The Structuralist Activity" appears twice in these books (and I admit to using it in my own *Critical Theory Since Plato*), but it is a weak essay and gives little idea of Barthes's work.[4] Jakobson on metonymy is an important essay, and Poulet's "Phenomenology of Reading" is perhaps an obvious choice. One of the books before me has Heidegger on Hölderlin; another does not. Derrida and Lacan appear only in the Johns Hopkins symposium and there rather unsatisfactorily.[5] Of course, they are not strictly literary theorists, but neither were Plato and Kant.

The problem with the anthological presentation of criticism is often the failure to get at the intellectual presuppositions of those not necessarily—at the moment—focusing on literary texts or even on literature, if literature exists, which is one of the ideas that the *nouvelle critique* calls into doubt.[6] Anthologies often leave theoretical questions unplumbed in the welter of discourse that they offer. One senses in these books a babble of tongues and in many cases, worse, a jangling of jargon unapproached even in the early days of the American New Criticism. This in spite of Barthes's idea

---

2 *The New Apologists for Poetry* (Minneapolis: Univ. of Minnesota Press, 1956).

3 *Structuralist Poetics: Structuralism, Linguistics and the Study of Literature* (Ithaca: Cornell Univ. Press, 1975).

4 It appears in Gras, pp. 157-63; Polletta, pp. 123-28. The latter also includes Barthes's essay on *Phèdre*, and the former another section of his work on Racine.

5 Roman Jakobson, "Two Aspects of Language: Metaphor and Metonymy," in Gras, pp. 119-29; Georges Poulet, "Phenomenology of Reading," in Polletta, pp. 103-18; Martin Heidegger, "Hölderlin and the Essence of Poetry," in Gras, pp. 27-41; Jacques Derrida, "Structure, Sign, and Play in the Discourse of the Human Sciences," in Macksey and Donato, pp. 247-72; Jacques Lacan, "Of Structure as an Inmixing of an Otherness Prerequisite to Any Subject Whatever," in Macksey and Donato, pp. 186-200.

6 See, for example, Alan Bass, " 'Literature'/Literature," in Macksey, pp. 341-53; and Jacques Derrida's remark, quoted by Bass, that "literature annihilates itself through its own illimitability" (*La Dissémination*, [Paris: Seuil, 1972], p. 253). On this point also note Tzvetan Todorov, "The Notion of Literature," *NLH*, 5, No. 1 (Autumn 1973), 5-16.

in "The Two Criticisms" that there are simply two types of critical approach—the academic and the new.[7] Barthes's essay, which was severely and notoriously attacked in France, appeared curiously provincial to an American when it was published in *MLN* in 1963. It seemed about twenty years out of date. The struggle Barthes was describing against the positivism of the academy in France had had its parallel in America in the thirties and early forties, though on different grounds. Barthes *sounded* like the American New Critics:

What [academic criticism] rejects is that this interpretation and this ideology may decide to work within an area purely internal to the work. In short, what is refused is *immanent analysis*; anything is acceptable so long as the work can be related to *something other* than itself, to something other than literature.[8]

As I have observed, even the concept "literature" is eventually called into question by the *nouvelle critique*, but up to this point Barthes's complaint appears very much like that of Blackmur in the well-known "A Critic's Job of Work" (1935), and the attack on positivism is familiar from the essays of Tate written about 1940.[9]

Yet there are very significant differences. Barthes concluded his essay by citing as among the "immanent" approaches rejected by the academic positivists the phenomenological, thematic, and structural. The first and third were virtually unknown when the American New Critics began to write, though they preached some aspects of both and certainly invented the second, which Barthes describes as a criticism that "reconstitutes the internal metaphors of a work."[10] Edward W. Said is surely correct when he regrets that the structuralists have been isolated from North American criticism.[11] He is also correct, I think, in stating, in spite of Barthes's simplifications, that structuralism is a kind of positivism in itself.[12]

---

[7] In Macksey, pp. 66-71.

[8] *Ibid.*, p. 70.

[9] See my *Critical Theory Since Plato* (New York: Harcourt Brace Jovanovich, 1971), pp. 892-904 for Blackmur, and pp. 928-41 for Tate's "Literature as Knowledge."

[10] The New Critics would, however, never have employed a word like "reconstitutes," for it would have seemed to them to indicate the dominance or superiority of the critical act over the work.

[11] See "*Abecedarium Culturae*: Structuralism, Absence, Writing," in Simon, pp. 372-73.

[12] *Ibid.*, p. 369.

I come away from a study of these contemporary movements with a sense that there are fundamental divisions among them not really conveyed by any of these anthologies. These differences are little understood, for they are coming to the surface here only slowly. Vernon Gras is helpful in this because he organizes his anthology in such a way as to separate "existential phenomenology" from "structuralism," the two movements being ideologically opposed when perceived in their purity. But there are mixtures in practice. Both structuralists and phenomenologists marvel sweetly over the mysteries of verbal mediation. Do we have as a result a "terrible beauty" being born? Or is it a "rough beast"?

What seems certain to me is that we are in danger of losing literature entirely in the so-called crisis of language that seems to have been created by our time. (The French literati do have a way of defining everything in crisis terms, don't they?) Criticism threatens to break down all boundaries and to rival (by obliteration) literature itself. There is something of the egotistical sublime in this that seems to render the structuralist critic, when terminally infected, incapable of getting outside the positivistic presuppositions of his own "ordinary" language. To call what he is doing the "science of man" does not hide the fact that the implicit attitudes toward language and art are those of the familiar *social* scientist. Some vestige of Keatsian empathy is lacking—the Keats who sought to peck around in the gravel with the sparrows.

At the other end of the scale is the phenomenological critic, whose godfather, Heidegger, seems sometimes to be the Germanic professor struggling in a curious no man's land between the dryness of metaphysical language and the language of the romantic poem. The French critic Poulet writes meditations or Mallarméan orations on poems. The American critic, Bloom, moves radically to obliterate distinctions and seeks miraculously to turn himself into a poet through criticism.

What is the old saying? First similarities, then differences? Or is it the other way around? No matter, both are necessary to communication, and the critic must balance them. This requires that he look at literature from its own point of view, even as he knows that he must maintain *his* point of view as well. I think the structuralists and phenomenologists fail in this, but at opposite extremes. The anthologies do not bring this problem to light, but perhaps some further study can. Rather than the compromise or mediation between them suggested by Gerald R. Bruns in a recent interesting book, [13] what is needed is an independent position aware of but free of the recent efforts of Gallic rationality. I do not think this position can be one arising out of Wittgensteinian language analysis, so well studied by M. H. Abrams. [14] Here, too, it seems to me that the attitude toward language does not escape the positivistic. The poem's own formal attitude toward itself is not given adequate play.

Both Giambattista Vico early in the eighteenth century and Ernst Cassirer early in the twentieth, speak of the difficulty and yet the necessity, for their endeavors, of trying to see something from its own point of view. In *The New Science*, Vico remarks of the difficulty of coming to understand the way human thinking arose in and as "poetic logic." He tells us that he expended twenty years in the effort to understand that development from inside itself: "We had to descend from these human and refined natures of ours to those quite wild and savage natures, which we cannot at all imagine and can comprehend only with great effort." [15] Cassirer observes, "We cannot reduce myth to certain fixed static elements; we must strive to grasp it in its inner life, in its mobility and diversity, in its dynamic principle." [16] The problem with respect to poetry is the same as that with myth: even the most careful of discursive approaches betrays an alien perspective. Cassirer himself is an example. Much as Cassirer insists on the empathetic principle, he proceeds from a treatment of myth to discussions of language and art, distinguishing between them while at the same time using the linguistic art of poetry among examples of art. His opposition between language and art is unwittingly contradicted by these examples, and poetry is left unaccounted for. Language for him, after all, is language as it has purged itself of myth and is purifying itself in the direction of mathematics. He does not fully rid himself of the tendency to see literary art strictly from the perspective of such ideal discourse, because for him language is to be defined

---

[13] Gerald R. Bruns, *Modern Poetry and the Idea of Language* (New Haven: Yale Univ. Press, 1974).

[14] "What's the Use of Theorizing about the Arts," in Bloomfield, pp. 1-54.

[15] *The New Science of Giambattista Vico*, rev. trans. of the 3rd ed. of 1744, trans. T. G. Bergin and M. H. Fuch (Ithaca: Cornell Univ. Press, 1968), p. 100.

[16] Ernst Cassirer, *An Essay on Man* (New Haven: Yale Univ. Press, 1944), p. 76.

from the point of view of its own state of ideal perfectibility—the end of a long development toward abstract purity. There is here a submerged eschatology that envisions perfectibility of a certain sort. This eschatology, which we can rightly call positivistic, wars with Cassirer's respect for myth, estranges language from art, and poetry, if it is to be regarded as an art, from language. It forces the very struggle that Cassirer wants to avoid.

Vico's struggle is with the received notion of tropes. In classical parlance, tropes are deviations from normal language, and the trace of this concept persists in Vico's description of the tropological nature of "poetic logic," even though Vico's point is that in his primitive "poetic logic," which is comparable to Cassirer's "mythical thought," tropes were not in any sense deviant but fundamental to the way language creates itself and its thought. This attitude toward tropes as deviant recurs in the language of contemporary structuralism and makes a perspective even partly from inside poetry theoretically difficult—almost, I think, impossible—for the structuralists. Among them, too, Saussure's terminology of *signifiant* and *signifié*, which assumes in language a certain relation or disrelation between word and concept, requires when poetry is the subject, the fabrication of a terminology—difference, nothingness, etc.—to express the absence of a conventionally or substantially conceived *signifié*. Indeed, among some critics the idea of language as creative of such *signifié* as it has, or any concept of language as fundamentally "poetic," is dismissed as requiring "demystification" or reduction to terms compatible with a fundamentally classical or rationalistic norm of discourse. The problem of self-contradiction in Cassirer and what might be called terminological barbarism in the structuralists arises from unstated assumptions about language that may be described as positivistic and anti-artistic in spite of the interests and values professed on the surfaces of these discourses. But pursuit of this matter must be somewhat delayed at this point.

In the face of a dominant rationalism, particularly on the continent generated by Descartes, there was a struggle waged by certain theorists, and it was dominated by defensive tactics from Baudelaire through Mallarmé to Valéry. They tried to make the case for poetry in a language dominated by the enemy. In employing that language in a straightforward way the literary theorist finds himself driven either to speak in paradoxes (such as the resort to "silence") or finally to hold extreme positions that impose severe limits on the cultural role of art. Most such efforts have failed somewhere—maybe have necessarily failed—because they do not sustain an almost impossible linguistic rigor and irony.

The position I would present is not now fashionable. Though it has some affinities with structuralism, it regards structuralism as captured by positivism. It has some sympathy with modern phenomenological criticism, but departs from its basic philosophical attitudes by recourse not to Heidegger but to a Cassirer purged of the contradictions I have mentioned. One of its own fundamental ideas is that, as Herder and von Humboldt concluded, language is constitutive of thought. Thought does not precede linguistic formulation but takes form in it, form being more than mere appearance, shape, or order, and not a term opposed to "content." Concepts are therefore linguistic. Von Humboldt says, "Languages are not really means for representing already known truths but are rather instruments for discovering previously unrecognized ones." [17] But language is not really an instrument to *look through*; it is radically creative and "no object is possible without it for the psyche." [18] One could go so far as to say that concepts inhere *in* and *as* language. They are not something that language copies or represents (for then they would precede language), nor are they properly regarded as separate from language once they have been created by, in, and as language. However, even though concepts are creations inside and as the very form of language, language hypostasizes concepts and fictionalizes an apartness for them. This is what I have called elsewhere the creation of "antimyth"—the fictive projection to an "outside" of something language really has inside itself, followed by the fiction that the outside preceded its containing substance. [19] It seems to me that von Humboldt was struggling toward some such idea when he wrote:

The least advantageous influence on any sort of interesting treatment of linguistic studies is exerted by the narrow notion that language originated as a

---

[17] Wilhelm von Humboldt, *Humanist Without Portfolio: An Anthology of the Writings of Wilhelm von Humboldt*, trans. Marianne Cowan (Detroit: Wayne State Univ. Press, 1963), p. 246.

[18] *Ibid.*, p. 293.

[19] See my "Blake and the Philosophy of Literary Symbolism," *NLH*, 5, No. 1 (Autumn 1973), 135-46.

convention and that words are nothing but signs for things or concepts which are independent of them. This view up to a point is certainly correct but beyond this point it is deadly because as soon as it begins to predominate it kills all mental activity and exiles all life. [20]

I would declare that it cannot be said (except with the reservation that it can be said self-consciously as a fiction) that *signifiants* signify anything. The terminology of *signifiant* and *signifié* is, at this level, of value only inside the linguistic fiction that hypostasizes concept or meaning. The structuralists perhaps recognize this in their insistence that *signifiants* signify only difference between words, not concepts or what we normally think of as *signifiés*. Difference for them is the empty space or nothingness between words that ultimately makes no word adequate to the expression of a concept. Structuralism, bereft of a true *signifié*, finds it necessary to construct the fiction of this void between words, this nothingness, as a something because it is tied to the assumptions implicit in its original terms: a *signifiant* must have a *signifié*, if only a *signifié* declared to be an absence.

I hesitate to claim that structuralist theory here is merely sound and fury, but it does claim that signifiers signify nothing. Structuralist terminology always tends to turn terms we employ in common speech inside out. A long list could be created: signifiers do not signify, deconstruction is a new construction, demystification creates a new mystery, difference implies similarity, and so on. This is structuralism's own exhibition of irony and of a new and not always acknowledged mystery. It has always been the fate of criticism to say one thing and to mean another; the question is whether or not structuralist ironies and mysteries are the best we can expect or whether they are not examples of a polysemous perversity from which we shall all, after the first great wave, require deliverance. I observe here only that such acrobatics reflect, for me, at least, the inability of language, when pure abstraction and logical purity in the guise of ordinariness is regarded as its norm, to cope with its own linguistic art.

The reason this occurs is that structuralist discussion of poetry proceeds—as so much discussion of poetry has traditionally proceeded—from deeply ingrained assumptions that words copy things and if, as in Plato, things themselves are copies, then words

---

[20] Von Humboldt, p. 249.

copy ideas, or words copy their meanings. It is amazing how thoroughly this point of view dominates the discourses even of those structuralists who profess not to believe it. In apparently trying to get at this point, von Humboldt distinguished poetry from prose, but ever so tentatively:

The characteristic difference between poetry and prose ... is that prose declares by its form that it wishes to accompany and serve. Poetry cannot do without at least appearing to control thought or actually bringing it forth. [21]

The prose-poetry distinction seems inadequate to us today, some prose having declared its alliance with the poem, but there are two important attitudes implicit in von Humboldt's description. The endless play of the possible relation or disrelation of *signifiant* and *signifié* that we find in the work of Jacques Derrida and his coining of the term *différance*, where the *signifié* becomes only the result of the process of interpretation, comes at the whole problem of poetry from the point of view of what von Humboldt above calls prose. This play is perhaps more than what Kenneth Burke calls "good showmanship," but it never breaks out of itself into real engagement with literature. Derrida does not, of course, pretend that it does, but his influence spreads to those who would have it do so if it could, or they would abolish "literature." Whether there is any way to produce any other result from this insistent prosaicism and Gallic rationality is uncertain.

But what if it is possible, taking Vico's lead, to begin with the idea that "poetic logic," if not historically prior, is logically prior to other logics built upon it, or, in a terminology I shall use, projected outward from it? Historical priority is claimed by Vico for his "poetic logic" and by Cassirer for his primordial unity of language and myth, "myth, language and art being as a concrete, undivided unity, which is only gradually resolved into a triad of individual modes of spiritual creativity." [22] But Cassirer's assertion, like so many modern assertions, draws a line at some unspecified historical point in every culture. Before, all is one. Afterward, language, myth, and art are forever separated. This has led to efforts to rescue literary art from language, in Cassirer's ideal,

---

[21] *Ibid.*, p. 218.
[22] Ernst Cassirer, *Language and Myth*, trans. Susanne K. Langer (New York: Harper and Brothers, 1946), p. 98.

eschatological sense of the term. We are well aware of the many theories of absolute opposition between literature and ordinary language, between "depth language" and "steno language" (as in Philip Wheelwright), [23] and so on.

I wish to accept the logical priority of "poetic logic" and something I shall provisionally call "poetic language," but I am not prepared to proclaim an absolute fissure between poetic language and any such language as might be set up in opposition to it. Instead I wish to admit the possibility of a continuum of language from a poetic center outward. At the end of his *Anatomy of Criticism*, Northrop Frye speculates about the relation of poetry to mathematics, though it is clear that in fundamental respects they hold radically different places on such a continuum. [24] Yet paradoxically they meet, too. The continuum I propose is an unmeasurable one running from a poetic center, with all the priority that implies, outward through the zone of ordinary language, if it exists, through the area of Wheelwright's "steno language" to mathematical symbolism, which marks the outer circumference of symbolic creativity. We may, as we proceed, have reason to believe that William Blake's ultimate identification of true centers with circumferences may apply here; that is, the center really contains all the possibilities implicit in the totality.

It should be clear that this priority of the poetic center absolutely reverses the assumptions about language upon which modern social science bases its methods, since modern social science with its quantitative assumptions places mathematics at the center, building abstract models of human behavior outward from it. Before most structuralist criticism has begun, it has made assumptions about the language of poetry that are diametrically opposed to placement of such a thing as a "poetic logic" at a center.

If we are to make the effort to adopt or even acknowledge (since adoption may finally be impossible) the point of view of the centrality of "poetic logic," from which all things proceed (and to which they return?), we must rethink what can appropriately be

---

[23] *The Burning Fountain: A Study in the Language of Symbolism*, rev. ed. (Bloomington: Indiana Univ. Press, 1968). See esp. chapter 5, "Traits of Expressive Language."

[24] *Anatomy of Criticism* (Princeton: Princeton Univ. Press, 1957), pp. 350-52.

said about poetry. For example, we can hardly declare tropes to be deviations from some norm. From this point of view, the idea of discourse, which eliminates all tropes in asserting a norm that is really an ideal of pure mathematic abstraction, is the real deviation, or, to put it better, the movement outward from the center of language. Metaphor, metonymy, and the rest are not, at the center, merely devices to lend vividness to argument or to entertain. The ideal of such purification toward the bare bones of logic, culminating in mathematics, is, of course, derived from assumptions about how the mind works. Rather than computers being made to copy the mind, the mind is declared to be a copy of a computer. The concept of "ordinary language," so popular among analytical philosophers, becomes confused with the ideal abstract mathematic concept of language.

The point that there is no ordinary language has been cleverly made by Stanley Fish, who attacks the distinction between ordinary and literary language by declaring the nonexistence of both. [25] My commentary here has proceeded along somewhat different lines from his, but it acknowledges that the radical distinction between something called literary and other language has been a millstone around the neck of criticism, though it seems that it was one that for a time—as a defensive measure—had to be worn. The construction of a fictive concept of literary language as special or privileged (par excellence in the theorizing of Paul Valéry) was a defensive maneuver against an oppressive cultural force, but it has played into the hands of the positivistic opponent by adopting the same sense of normality as is everywhere in positivism. Ordinary language seems to me a misleading fiction useless to criticism as long as it is employed to declare poetry in some way deviant. To insist on deviance in this situation is to establish an unmoving center. It is a dead center like Dante's Satan and devours poetry by varieties of reduction.

Fish argues that the distinction has forced criticism to claim that poetry is either more than language (message plus, or the "surplus" of the structuralists), which leads to a concept of decorative form, or less than language (message minus), which eliminates content and gives us theories of "pure poetry." This situation does exist as long as we define the center of language as conveyance of

---

[25] "How Ordinary is Ordinary Language?" *NLH,* 5, No. 1 (Autumn 1973), 41-54.

a message, not creation of thought that is one with itself. But Fish's analysis does not focus finally on the issue that is fundamental for my purposes. That is, whether language is creative or only imitative, formative of thought or only representative of it. To Vico's "poetic logic" I want to add the characteristic of symbolic formation. I am not content with a poetic logic that claims the mythic (as in Cassirer's mythical thought) identity of word and thing or with the transparency (as in Michel Foucault's Renaissance thought) of words, leading to things. [26]

With poetic logic as the center, tropes are no longer tropes in the classical sense. In the classical view there must always be a gap between word and concept. There is always a possible improvement by substitution. Language is never quite adequate to what it wants to represent. This classical idea of the relation or disrelation of word to concept is what led the romantic period to generate a special derogatory meaning for "allegory." On the other hand, if we regard a word as generating in itself a concept, the concept is not an otherness, and the word does not "signify" in the ordinary sense of this term. The structuralists attempt to make the term "signify" ironic by claiming the signification to be of nothing or difference.

According to my view, language projected along the continuum from center to mathematic circumference came to create the verbal fiction of the nonverbal concept or pure idea. But this fiction, apart from language, has no more substance than the Kantian thing-in-itself, for it is always created *from* and *in* words. We cannot as critics (without totally abandoning respect for the point of view of the poem) drive language outward into a situation where it is merely approximating a preceding nonverbal idea.

Instead of the problem of words and concepts, which has been the domain of the structuralists, what about words and things? Phenomenologists tell us we must get back to things and free ourselves of the tyrannical abstractness of words and ideas. But this, too, presumes the existence of the norm of language far out from the poetic center. On the contrary, we must affirm that things are not simply just "as they are" but that the imagination has a hand in constructing them and that this construction is with and in language. From this point of view the imagination is

---

26 Michel Foucault, *The Order of Things (Les mots et les choses)* (New York: Random House, 1973), esp. pp. 17-44.

linguistic (or symbolic, to include other "languages"), and one may well ask, What are things apart from the form which man gives to them via his symbolizing? They are merely a pure potentiality. This is to say that a world prior to the human fiat lacks full reality or is unfinished, and that the real is something we *proceed to make* rather than *refer back or outward toward*. The reality we claim to reach out to beyond our forms is, from this point of view, a will-o'-the-wisp, a nightmare caused, as Blake insists, by our looking in the wrong direction. To have created the "antimyth" of the abstract otherness or objectivity of the world as the exclusive reality is to have created a symbolic structure that projects such a world and ignores all else. This is exactly what Blake's Urizen does, and in doing it he creates hell and becomes Satan himself.

I choose, borrowing from Vico and Cassirer, to seek a theory of radical creativity in language that gives priority to the poetic. In this attempt I adopt the term "symbolic" roughly in Cassirer's sense. But the term "symbol" presents something of the same problem for me as *signifiant* does for the structuralist. Benedetto Croce was quite right to ask what a symbol, used in this sense, symbolizes. [27] Rather than re-creating the distance between *signifiant* and *signifié*, I employ symbolization to indicate an act of linguistic creativity with and in language. For the symbol, there is no symbolized, only the realm of the potential to be worked up into the symbol. In Croce's terms, this, of course, involves the identity of intuition and expression. Being is not prior to, but the result of, language.

I give to man the creation of language in the manner of Blake's "ancient poets," whom Blake declares to have confronted a pure potentiality and set about making by naming the world. Today each of us grows up in a language that, like Blake's eternal London, is constantly decaying even as it is being built. True, as continental criticism likes to tell us, we cannot recapture purity. We have the endless task of retrieving language from its own tendency toward ruin. But if *creation* does not go on as decay takes place, the world of human culture, which is the real world, decays and becomes hell. Hell is the diminishment of culture, the result of human passivity.

My view directs us radically toward the future, not toward

---

27 *Guide to Aesthetics*, trans. Patrick Romonell (Indianapolis: Bobbs-Merrill Co., 1965), p. 23.

the individual death that is the one reality of the existentialists, but toward the continuing act of linguistic creation, toward a passing along of the cultural role. It restores the literal root meaning of "poet." However, it connects the maker not merely with the poet as conventionally conceived but with all who symbolize, including those makers who seem to be taking apart but actually are constructing antimyth. It becomes clear, from this point of view, for example, that history, which seems directed toward an outward past, is the act of creating that past, a symbolic past, which is the only past we have. We are always thus on the threshold of history in an entirely different sense from the common one. We are always making it.

The difference between *signifiant* and *signifié* is itself a fictive creation in language as it operates at a distance from the poetic center, beyond that unlocatable point where poetic logic has turned into antimyth. To look back from this vantage to the poem is to submit it to a mode of thought that appears to be the poem's contrary, where the poem is declared to require interpretation and to hide a *meaning*, where the poem is, in romantic terms, an allegory. But these are all characterizations finally not of the poem but of the limitations of this point of view toward the poem. This point of view, somewhere outward from the center toward mathematics, is in the area of the positivistic, where language itself invents the dislocations that we, when we stand *there*, thrust back upon poems.

As I have said, this area appears to be purely the opposite of the poetic and locked in an endless contrariety with it. Cassirer at the end of *An Essay on Man* found it so. [28] I myself have so treated it, and in a sense it is true; [29] but such treatment erects a too hard-and-fast opposition, declares an absolutely and simply located point of difference on the continuum, thrusts us back into an awkward distinction between ordinary and literary, steno and depth language, and overspatializes and quantifies the unmeasurable continuum between center and circumference.

I propose that this whole continuum is radically creative, but that as we pass further and further outward, what we create is the fiction or antimyth of externality—until we reach mathematics,

---

[28] Cassirer, *An Essay on Man*, p. 228.
[29] In my "Yeats, Dialectic and Criticism," *Criticism*, 10, No. 3 (Summer 1968), 185-99.

where something very strange happens, for mathematics proceeds to assert its power to contain, claims that the world is mathematical rather than that mathematics represents the world. In any case, we see that our continuum defies measurement and that we cannot even say where poetry ceases and another form of language begins, where antimyth replaces myth, though we do know by our own declarations when it is that we face a poem.

The adoption of the terms *signifiant* and *signifié* as applicable to the whole continuum of language is, from the point of view of the center, a betrayal of poetry. It is a reduction of everything to a positivistic perspective. From the center, poetry is not an aspect of language, but language is a constant growing out from poetry, though still tied to it. This is why William Blake claimed that the sort of center I have been discussing is the real circumference—an expanding center—a container of all possibility. If the perspective shifts outward, then poetry becomes escapist fantasy or decorated messages, or lamentation over the failure of language to overcome difference or to get back to things.

It is true, of course, that if we are to talk about poetry, criticism must, because it projects itself farther out on the radius than any poem it treats, employ the categories of analysis and reduction. Criticism, increasingly aware of its situation, tends in our own time to find its own predicament as interesting as—sometimes more interesting than—poetry itself. It tends, as in some recent continental work, to project itself inward from itself and treat its own activity as a poem to be interpreted. A certain amount of this is to be expected and is valuable as a built-in check against irresponsibility, but it has its serious dangers—the possibility of infinite regress, the tendency, as one projects one's critical stance farther and farther out, to deaden analysis into more and more reductive quantitative procedures, or the loss of the poem in the narcissism of the critical act. Criticism is most effective when its analytic procedures are observed with a certain skepticism and the irony of its place is fully acknowledged. From the point of view of the poetic center, it is criticism that is ironic, not the poem. The old opposition of art and science catches criticism in the middle of the continuum, that unmeasurable area where neither term seems quite to fit. From this odd perch, irony is one of the things criticism projects back into poetry when criticism's own language cannot hold the poem together in any other way. We as critics project the discontinuities of allegory into poems because these fissures are *our* condition. It should be no surprise that the self-regarding activity of continental criticism should valorize allegory. To do so is for it to justify itself. But this takes us back to a conclusion already reached that criticism is finally, like all symbolic forms, a *making* of its own. It makes an antimyth of bifurcations even when professing to seek out a unity in the poem. It is involved in a both-and situation like the dream as Freud imagined it. The danger to criticism is to lose its own sense of irony; to fail to remember that the poem has a point of view.

It is necessary here to state that the theory of radical creativity, though it refuses to draw a line *measuring off* poetry from other forms of discourse and argues for the creativity of all language, does not quarrel with our needs as critics to create an ironic fictive opposition where a continuum is the reality. Nor does it, in claiming the radical creativity of language, deny that language projects the antimyth of human passivity and automatism—the undesirable floor of things (against which we warn ourselves in language)—old chaos and ancient night. Even antimyth—the world of linguistic bondage and frustration, of subject and object—is a necessary projection if only to impel us toward renewed creativity. Blake called it the "starry floor" beneath which, through God's mercy, man could not fall. Much language is in the process of dying, and much language that is thought to be near the poetic center in one age is found to be dead by another. But the source of even our automatic language and the language we perceive being slaughtered around us was and is the poetic center. This is not to deny that many distinctions must be made—though ironically made—along the continuum, lest the term "literature" disappear in my system as it threatens to in structuralism, all discourse swallowed by poetry rather than all poetry swallowed by discourse. This is the problem Murray Krieger saw clearly some years ago in a neo-Kantian theory. [30]

I take seriously, then, the effort that emerges in romanticism to establish the idea of the symbol, no matter how halting, lacking in rigor, and full of lost opportunities and dead ends individual efforts to develop a theory of poetry out of it may have been. The distinction between allegory and symbolism marks the first step toward a wrenching of these terms from their tropological mean-

---

[30] *A Window to Criticism: Shakespeare's Sonnets and Modern Poetics* (Princeton: Princeton Univ. Press, 1964), pp. 57-58.

ings or their references to devices in a poem (their classical context) and toward reference to poems as wholes in the light of the creative powers of language as it operates at its own center. The distinction was therefore the first step toward a theory of symbolic forms, and it was one of the first toward a theory of fictions. Rather than regarding the distinction as mystification, I regard it as a positive effort in theory, even though it certainly did arise in part as a desperate defensive maneuver against dominant materialist orientations.

To trace the development of the theory of symbolism [31] along these lines would be to seek an appropriate description of literature's cultural role. I believe that role was inadequately stated in the New Criticism and has been obfuscated in modern continental criticism. Anglo-American criticism has never been very patient with the search for philosophical foundations. Modern continental criticism has been so concerned with philosophy—laboring for the most part in the immense shadow of Descartes—that it has often remained satisfied with its own self-regarding philosophical activity at the expense of the poem. (It is not surprising that it is from this tradition that the death of literature is proclaimed.) Of course, there have been exceptions on both sides, but I believe this characterization is helpful as a beginning. Anglo-American criticism has been a mixture of skepticism and pragmatism floating atop the influence of Kant. These tendencies have frequently been noted by commentators, but less often by the dominant critics themselves. (John Crowe Ransom did write on Kant, though somewhat eccentrically.) But Anglo-American criticism has not wanted to philosophize past a certain point, struggling as a matter of principle to maintain theoretical independence. Thus Kenneth Burke declares himself willing to employ any insight that will help him on the way, and Northrop Frye deliberately draws back at the end of his *Anatomy of Criticism* from engaging fully the philosophical questions his speculations seem to raise. There is a reason for this that requires at least a measure of respect. It is that Anglo-American critics tend to maintain a reticence about any criticism beginning from an abstract philosophical position and demanding judgment from that point of view. It is a reticence expressing profound respect for that unmeasurable distance between criticism and the poem. Yet I am not satisfied with its

---

[31] As I am trying to do in a work in progress.

hesitation to explore its own assumptions, and I do not rest easily with its pragmatism.

On the other hand, modern continental criticism has been Cartesian and subjectivist in its orientation, and existential in its play with *angst*. It has assumed a philosophical situation that it requires literature and those who write about it (or about themselves thinking about it) to endorse, all else—including the theory of symbolism—being mystification. The critic seems tempted to compete with his texts, to surpass them, and in his most ebullient moods, as I have noted, to deny the existence of literature entirely.

Among work written in English attacking the concept of the symbol, as it was developed out of romanticism, that of Paul de Man is perhaps best known. "Literary History and Literary Modernity" reveals his position *vis à vis* language:

> The writer's language is to some degree the product of his own action; he is both the historian and the agent of his own language. The ambivalence of writing is such that it can be considered both an act and an interpretive process that follows after an act with which it cannot coincide. [32]

However, of these two concepts of writing, it is the latter that dominates his work and continental criticism at this time. In another essay, both ingenious and influential, called "The Rhetoric of Temporality," he regards the concept of the symbol as a "mystification" that threw the romantics into irresolvable contradictions. [33] It is important to pay attention to this argument, since in the present ebullience of the continental spirit, it threatens to sweep all before it. Its emphasis is entirely different from that of the position I am taking. De Man declares that continental criticism "represents a methodologically motivated attack on the notion that a literary or poetic consciousness is in any way a privileged consciousness, whose use of language can pretend to escape, to some degree, from the duplicity, the confusion, the untruth that we take for granted in the everyday use of language."

---

[32] In Bloomfield, p. 250.

[33] Paul de Man, "The Rhetoric of Temporality," in *Interpretation: Theory and Practice*, ed. Charles S. Singleton (Baltimore: Johns Hopkins Press, 1969).

For de Man "unmediated expression" is a "philosophical impossibility." [34]

Lurking beneath both statements is the classical attitude that language is best described as a copier of a preceding reality and is best definable in terms of its use as conveyor of a message. The emphasis is *not* laid upon language as a maker and container of thought. For de Man, language stands between man and a hidden meaning that it can never fully express. From the point of view that I am taking, this meaning is a creation of language, which hypostasizes it, though in truth such meaning continues to inhere in language, and self-consciously so when language operates at its poetic center. The further out from that center language operates, the further outside of itself it tends to appear to thrust its so-called meaning. At the center it declares its meaning to be itself or interchanges the concept of meaning for that of being. But for de Man, there is no poetic center; language is a system of signs radically cut off from meaning:

It is the distinct privilege of language to be able to hide meaning behind a misleading sign, as when we hide rage or hatred behind a smile. But it is the distinctive curse of all language, as soon as any kind of interpersonal relation is involved, that it is forced to act this way.

Here the problem of *communication* is essential. I, on the other hand, take the possibility of *creation* as so. This is a critical difference in perspective that has epistemological implications and from which all our subsequent differences proceed. There is no doubt in my mind that communication is faulty, but it does not necessarily follow that language is inevitably a faulty means of conceptualization as making. De Man holds that the actual expression always fails to "coincide with what has to be expressed," [35] while I claim that a poem is first of all a making, not a copying or representation. Indeed, de Man goes so far as to reverse entirely this notion, proclaiming that in the word "fiction" is an admission or self-conscious awareness of the fact that no expression fully reveals meaning. My own view is that the term "fiction" emphasizes that something has been made rather than faultily copied. But de Man argues:

---

[34] Paul de Man, *Blindness and Insight* (New York: Oxford Univ. Press, 1971), p. 9.

[35] *Ibid.*, p. 11.

That sign and meaning can never coincide, is what is precisely taken for granted in the kind of language we call literary. Literature, unlike everyday language, begins on the far side of this knowledge; it is the only form of language free from the fallacy of unmediated expression. All of us know this, although we know it in the misleading way of wishful assertion of the opposite. Yet the truth emerges in the foreknowledge we possess of the true nature of literature when we refer to it as *fiction*. [36]

Several remarks are pertinent here. It is curious for de Man to insist that we seem only to declare this to be true by stating the opposite. It is interesting that the word "fiction" has spread its influence into areas other than literature—physics, for example, where it clearly is identified with creation or making of a thought. But the fundamental observation I want to make here is that the passage says that language vainly attempts to communicate a fully preexistent meaning, that language and thought do not create, and that a "fiction" is a deviation from an established reality or meaning (though how this is possible if we cannot ever arrive at meaning is unclear). De Man's and my emphases may appear merely logically independent, but there is a fundamental disagreement between us about the role of language in thought, the nature of the imagination, and, indeed, the human condition.

I deal with de Man's position at some length because it is a common one in contemporary criticism influenced by structuralism and phenomenology, even when skeptically held. (Witness de Man's colleague, Geoffrey H. Hartman, who calls tropes "imaginative substitution" while worrying similar problems of mediation, tiptoe gingerly around de Man's position in an interesting but finally inconclusive review of *Blindness and Insight*.) [37] The difference of orientation between continental criticism and the theory I would like to develop is well displayed, as I have implied, by contrasting the valorization of symbolism in my position and that of allegory in de Man's. In approaching this matter, de Man points out, "Hans-Georg Gadamer makes the valorization of symbol at the expense of allegory coincide with the growth of an aesthetic that refuses to distinguish between experience and the representation of this experience." [38] This is the common distinction and works well

<hr>

36 *Ibid.*, p. 17.
37 *The Fate of Reading* (Chicago: Univ. of Chicago Press, 1974), p. 97 and pp. 308-12.
38 De Man, "The Rhetoric of Temporality," p. 174.

enough for the use of these terms in romanticism, but it does not
do justice to modern developments in the tradition with which I
am concerned, where the distinction that is obliterated or at least
softened is one between experience and the verbal *formation*, not
the *representation*, of it.

With Gadamer, de Man goes on to treat the symbol as something with indefiniteness of meaning. This is all right, except that
priority in his analysis is given to a clear meaning. By the very way
he puts the issue, the symbol is made to be a representation of a
previously existent meaning, rather than the other way around,
where the symbol forms its own meaning. Indefiniteness of meaning is for de Man always to be deplored. It is mystification, weak
thought. It is, in fact, a debasement of allegory, which properly
expresses the relation of sign to meaning. A symbol can only be,
to use Fish's terms, "message minus." But what if this indefiniteness of meaning is really a sign in itself of the inevitable failure of
a naive theory of interpretation to reach an assumed preexistent
meaning that has never really existed—consequently a failure to
reach the poem? The huge commentary in modern criticism about
the impossibility of translation and the "heresy" of paraphrase
argues in favor of this view.

The symbol in de Man, as in most of the *nouvelle critique*, is
treated as a trope, and a very inadequate trope at that, for it can
never deliver on its promises. Now there is considerable truth to
this position if one examines much romantic *practice*, and I do not
quarrel with this evidence; but I prefer to consider romantic *theory*
of the symbol as a searching in the direction of a description of
the poem as a whole, where the characteristics of the so-called
trope "symbol" are ultimately seen as pertaining not to a device or
element in the poem but to the poem as a whole. De Man's
treatment of irony as a trope is in the same way completely
different from that of the American New Critics who came to use
the term as descriptive of whole poems rather than of parts of
poems. [39]

---

[39] Interestingly enough, de Man's position on this point has something in
common with the critique of the American New Critics made by the Chicago
neo-Aristotelians some years ago. They complained that the New Critics made
one characteristic of a poem (possession of the trope irony) into a sign of
the poetic quality of the poem—an essence. What really happens in Cleanth
Brooks's "Irony as a Principle of Structure" is a wrenching of the term
"irony" out of the classical rhetorical vocabulary to be used as a term

By the same process the romantics made allegory a term that means "nonpoem." What de Man must see as supremely important—the *meaning* of the poem—is what the romantics called "allegory" and what to them and later critics became the hated paraphrase. The confusion that resulted was twofold: First, poems containing allegory as it was traditionally understood were routinely denigrated when disliked, even though it is difficult to find a major poem that does not contain allegory in this sense. Second, the term "symbol," on its way to becoming a term for a poem, kept slipping back to its usage as designating a special sort of trope with miraculous powers. This can be said to have led to much flying off into what T. E. Hulme called the "circumambient gas." [40] Insofar as de Man is complaining about this sort of miraculism in the so-called trope called the symbol, I am with him. It is another language in which to complain about romantic sentimentality. It is also regrettable that in making the term "allegory" mean nonpoem there was no term left available to criticism to describe, let alone do justice to, traditional allegorical usage, or what I call the hypostasization of meaning. But these are not the issues of concern. When de Man attacks romantic theorists, he attacks them for valorizing the symbol as *trope*, while I see them as struggling with the classical terminology of tropes against its fundamental assumptions about poetic wholes and toward a new theory of poetic wholes. As so often occurs in the history of language, romantic critics appropriated, or in Kenneth Burke's term "stole," the terms of the old rhetorical criticism, wrenching them for their own uses. [41] Ultimately they were struggling to move from the idea that a poem contains symbols (and for that reason is valuable) to the view that the whole of a poem is a symbolic form.

In de Man and continental criticism there exists a continuation of that profound disillusionment with language that is one

---

describing the nature of the poem as a whole. In other words, Brooks does with "irony" what the romantics began to do with "symbolism," but both terms tend to slip back to their tropological meanings when critical discourses lose rigor.

[40] *Speculations*, ed. Herbert Read (1924; rpt. New York: Harcourt, Brace and Co., 1936), p. 120.

[41] This concept of linguistic theft is nicely expressed in Burke's *Attitudes Toward History*, The New Republic Series, 2 (New York: New Republic, 1937), 229.

dominant mood of romanticism. But there is another mood that continually seeks to formulate the full range of the possibilities of language. I do not believe it accurate to characterize this effort as "mystification." Rather than assuming, as de Man does, that Friedrich von Schlegel erred in substituting "symbol" for the term "allegory" in the later version of his "Gespräch über die Poesie," I believe that he was on the track of something. [42] The word may be an "alien presence" in the later version (though I doubt it), but that may be because the essay as a whole does not catch up with romantic thought.

Certainly romanticism was incomplete and in many respects abortive. E. E. Bostetter is correct in so viewing it:

What seems at first glance triumphant affirmation is revealed on close observation as a desperate struggle for affirmation against increasingly powerful obstacles. The ultimate impression left by the poetry is of gradual loss of vitality and confidence too easily won and precariously held; of diminishing faith in the power of man; of a growing gap between the material and the spiritual and a deepening doubt; of affirmation hardening into an incantatory rhetoric sharply at odds with the perceptions and experience it conveys. Romantic poetry becomes in part the testing of a syntax that proved inadequate to the demands placed upon it. [43]

Romanticism failed in these ways because it asked too much of language and was not content with considering what it is that language *can* do. Part of the failure stems from continuing to treat the symbol as a trope in the old classic sense while at the same time struggling toward a concept of the poetic whole as a symbolic form.

The turn in Coleridge from Kant to Schelling is perhaps indicative of romanticism's yearning for an ultimate. Kant was content to admit that thought could never achieve the thing-in-itself. De Man connects this yearning with the romantic concept of the symbol, which would be a vehicle supposedly to achieve the ultimate—a form of language transcending language. He sees Wordsworth renouncing the "seductiveness and the poetical resources of a symbolical diction" and turning to allegory. This retreat he thinks inevitable to any right-thinking poet, the union of *signifiant*

---

[42] De Man, "The Rhetoric of Temporality," pp. 175-76.
[43] *The Romantic Ventriloquists* (Seattle: Univ. of Washington Press, 1963), p. 5.

and *signifié*, subject and object, and so on, being impossible.
Further, for de Man, allegory is fundamentally temporal, in that an
allegorical sign refers always to a "previous sign with which it can
never coincide" in the enclosure which is language. "It is the
essence of this previous sign," he says, "to be pure anteriority." [44]
Here de Man draws on the continental existential tradition, from
which all he has to say follows: In a temporal system of allegorical
signs there is, from the point of view of any given moment or
word, only a regress back through an infinite series of escaping
meanings. The present can never capture the ultimate meaning.

Martin Heidegger, whose influence on de Man and the whole
movement is immense, seems to offer a fictive beginning for this
otherwise infinite regress. In his *Introduction to Metaphysics* there
is perhaps the best example of his characteristic etymologizing in
search of true meaning. [45] Commentators on Heidegger have complained about this apparently pedantic etymologizing, but it is not
merely a quirk of the professor. It is quite central to his whole
approach, which is fundamentally theological. He presses words
back to "origins," where it can be imagined that word and concept
were one. With the modern word "being," he reaches back past
Aquinas, Aristotle, and Plato all the way to Heraclitus and Par-
menides, where he restores a unity of meaning to the original
word, before it was, Osiris-like, torn apart. This modern Isis recon-
structs its meaning by deconstructing its history. The myth behind
all this is that of the single original word given by God to man,
which broke up in the Babel of tongues. Language thus represents
the condition of the Fall. Heidegger finds the primordial word to
have been radically creative, but the fallen word is a mere sign:

Naming does not come afterward, providing an already manifest essent with a
designation and a hallmark known as a word; it is the other way around:
originally an act of violence that discloses being, the word sinks from this
height to become a mere sign, and this sign proceeds to thrust itself before
the essent. [46]

For de Man, allegory faces up to the fact of the Fall and "desig-
nates primarily a distance in relation to its own origin, and,

44 De Man, "The Rhetoric of Temporality," p. 190.
45 *An Introduction to Metaphysics*, trans. Ralph Manheim (New Haven:
Yale Univ. Press, 1959), p. 105.
46 *Ibid.*, p. 172.

renouncing the nostalgia and the desire to coincide, it establishes its language in the void of this temporal difference." According to this view the authentic voice of romantic literature is not its optimistic voice but its ironic one, emphasizing failure to reach ultimate meaning.

The myth of past origin halting the infinite regress of meaning is balanced in the future, in the existentialist view, not by a myth of achievement but by the fact of death. This word, incidentally, is never uttered in de Man's account of romanticism, but it lurks unspoken. Indeed, this fact obliterates all other meaning. Every fallen word looms toward it—the one authenticity. Is it possible to find in romanticism some possibility besides the disillusionment attendant upon the desire to transcend earth and the fixation upon death? Perhaps such an effort will be called "mystification." But both extremes I have mentioned seem to me excessively centered upon what Blake called the "selfhood" and its attendant egoism. If the symbol could be purged of its connections with the effort at transcendence and if we could find in it a reasonably mundane creative principle—one that concerns itself concretely with human culture—perhaps what begins in romanticism could be declared to have outgrown the crises Bostetter sees in it.

The romantic period certainly did not invent the distrust of words that now dominates continental thought. Joyce Cary uttered a well-known truth when he declared that poets have complained about words for at least two thousand years. [47] The "dissociation of sensibility," which is in some versions a dissociation of word and thing, word and thought, word and meaning, has been located variously in time. T. S. Eliot located it in the seventeenth century, Heidegger (if I am right) in the very development of language, Blake in the appearance of a "priesthood" of interpreters, and recently Michel Foucault in modernism. [48] For Foucault, the Renaissance treated language as transparent identification with things; classicism (French neoclassicism) resolved the connection of language with things in the idea of representation, all language

---

[47] *Art and Reality: Ways of the Creative Process* (New York: Harper and Brothers, 1958), p. 16.

[48] T. S. Eliot, "The Metaphysical Poets," *Selected Essays 1917-1932* (New York: Harcourt, Brace and Co., 1932), p. 247; William Blake, in "The Marriage of Heaven and Hell" (see my "Blake and the Philosophy of Literary Symbolism," p. 136); Michel Foucault, *The Order of Things*, p. 44.

being discourse; modernism separates literature from discourse. Foucault's analysis disregards almost entirely the movement in England and America called romantic, where both transparency and representation begin to be treated as unsatisfactory, and language begins to be seen not merely as enclosure but as intimately involved with thought in cultural creation. Foucault is a Frenchman, and France had no Coleridge to deliver to it the news of Kant and the imagination. From the Anglo-American point of view, France went violently from the neoclassic to the modern. As a result there is classicism and then there is Mallarmé, the tradition of representation and discourse and then the withdrawal of literature from representation and signification into the aesthetic, where art is made deliberately to have no relation to things. In England, the intervening Romantic Movement struggled to assert for art an authority over things while at the same time trying to formulate the difference between art and neoclassical discourse.

English aestheticism is regarded in the Anglo-American tradition as a dead end. Its major product, W. B. Yeats, outgrew it. The shades of a positive romanticism persist in him. Mallarmé fights his battle in isolation. For him, it is a choice between the old neoclassicism, still alive on Parnassus, and the dominant scientistic positivism that has set the tone of modernism. Mallarmé chooses to practice a stately withdrawal and style of contempt. It is a brilliant tour de force, much to be admired, but finally it is an attempt to make something positive out of a negative act. Exercise of the modern French imagination has always required the acknowledgment of subjectivity. Exercise of the English imagination since Coleridge has always demanded a stirring toward encompassment of the objective. The presiding deity in the French situation is Descartes; that in the English is, through Coleridge, Kant.

But the romantic theory of imagination could not have developed and presaged its later forms without the special anxiety with which the question of words had come to be viewed. It took the threat of enclosure to raise the possibility of the specifically *linguistic* imagination. Though Bostetter rightly argues that romanticism for the most part failed through excessive claims, including claims for the imagination, it contained in itself the germ of a more modest cultural, rather than metaphysically transcendent, role for art. The French never had to fall from the dizzying heights of English romanticism, but neither did they ever rise to the achievement of a positive view of imaginative power directed

toward a specifically human culture. It is only such an achievement—recognized as occurring in language—that can truly free us
from both the old classicism and the old romanticism and the
positivistic strain of modernism that has emerged from them.

Perhaps at this point the most useful example of the romantic
distrust of language, created by one who claimed not to be a
romantic and judged romantic art to be "sickly," is the attitude of
Goethe's hero at the beginning of *Faust*. Faust's quarrel is with the
apparent impossibility of attaining to ultimate knowledge. His
resentment appears to be specifically against words and the para-
phernalia of science. Faust is first seen sitting in the gloom of his
cavernous study. He complains that his search for knowledge has
been a mere "rummaging around with words." [49] The study with
its books piled to the ceiling all around him has become an
enclosure. Faust is stirred to escape from it, but wherever he turns
he finds himself meditating on symbols that return him to himself.

The situation presented is crucially different from the Platonic
myth of another enclosure in the *Republic*, where Socrates incites
one to escape from the enclosure and its illusions through the
reason. It is different, too, from the later locked-in personality
deplored but accepted by Walter Pater, who, at the beginning of
the English Aesthetic Movement, declares not merely the impossibility of ultimate knowledge but the imprisonment of man in a
radical subjectivity that separates him totally from the world:
"Experience, already reduced to a group of impressions, is ringed
round for each one of us by that thick wall of personality through
which no real voice has ever pierced. . . ." [50] Goethe, whom
Schiller "proved" to be a romantic after all, [51] takes Faust beyond
this initial impasse to tragedy and in Part Two to accomplishment,
returning him to the world, where he becomes a builder of culture.
This conclusion reflects an element of vitality in Goethe, which he
possessed even to the end of a long career and which has placed
him beyond philosophical categorization. He is both classic and
romantic or neither. In his various pronouncements there is one
consistent thread, however, and that is the insistence on the poet's

---

[49] The phrase is from the C. F. MacIntyre translation (New York: New
Directions, 1949), p. 8.

[50] *The Renaissance* (New York: Boni and Liveright, 1919), p. 196.

[51] Friedrich von Schiller, "Conversations with Eckermann," in *Critical
Theory Since Plato*, p. 516

connection with the concrete and particular, with earth—the Virgin and Child are an excellent subject for art, not because of their religious significance, but because they are human. In *Faust*, he says, "It was . . . not in my line, as a poet to strive to embody anything *abstract*. . . ." [52] There are many problems in Goethe's pronouncements, but Goethe does verge on asserting a positive cultural role for poetry, moving from the negative enclosure of the Faustian study to establishment of the poetic power, not of transcendence, but of building on earth, presumably in language.

One apprehends a similar effort in Shelley's *Defense of Poetry*, though immensely complicated (and vitiated) by an attempt to place this cultural role in a Platonic context (where it does not fit) and by the presence of poems in the Shelley canon that lament even more desperately than Faust the enclosure of words—"Epipsychidion" and "Hymn to Intellectual Beauty," for example. Shelley locates imagination at a center and declares reason to be an emanation from it. He thinks of language "in the infancy of society" as poetry itself. He claims every "original language" to be itself the "chaos of a cyclic poem." [53] But he does not resolve satisfactorily any of the issues he raises about the relation of language to thought and to things, and he dissolves his essay at a crucial point into an unconvincing panegyric. Nevertheless, this one side of Shelley connects the poet to earth and to culture, placing the poet's function *here* rather than turning poetry into a complaint about failure to transcend the world, the expression of unquenchable metaphysical thirst.

What is the possibility of following out this impulse to see whether it can lead us neither to poetic language as a prison-house, where Gerald R. Bruns finds it displacing or arresting the function of signification, nor to poetic language as what he calls the "speech of the world," where the word destroys the antithesis of words and things by asserting transparence? [54] The line of pursuit I favor is the attempt to view the word as neither enclosure nor transparency revealing a preexisting thing or meaning, but as potentially creative of cultural reality, which is of the earth, but an earth of man's making and remaking in symbolic form.

---

[52]*Ibid.*, p. 515.

[53]Percy Bysshe Shelley, "A Defense of Poetry," in *Critical Theory Since Plato*, p. 500.

[54]Bruns, *Modern Poetry and the Idea of Language*, p. 262.

As you can see, though many regard as a terrible beauty the mixture of neo-romanticism and positivistic structuralism that is modern continental criticism and the emerging critical fashion in the anthologies under discussion, I am not sure that it is not a rough beast. If so, to extend the Yeatsianism, it belongs to a primary dispensation. Such periods are all right for hunchbacks, saints, and fools, but not for poets.

POSTSCRIPT*

By now, of course, I consider my essay, and not its subject, a rough beast, and I like to think of it ambling indifferently away from me, beyond recall or concern. When Professor Krieger asked me to write the essay, I was about two-thirds finished with a book manuscript called *The Philosophy of Literary Symbolism,* but I had written neither introduction nor conclusion. My essay became an attempt to find out where I was. The book will be an attempt to develop to its logical conclusions a theory of the symbolic; my essay was a striking out in that direction via a consideration principally of a tradition to which the concept of the symbolic has come to seem antithetical. It is a tradition involving both structuralists and phenomenologists, ending in an "allegoric" (to employ Blake's usage) conception of literature. The structuralist aspect is empirically allegoric and the phenomenological is religiously allegoric. Both are antimythical in the sense in which I have used the term.

I feel that the cultural role of literary art was well described by W. B. Yeats in his term "antithetical." This means that literary art is secular and humanistic—as the wars between philosophy and poetry, religion and poetry, and science and poetry have told us throughout history. But literature's antithetical nature is creative. Of course, the critics who would have us accept terrible beauty or rough beast would obliterate the opposition between literature and other discourse and subdue it to one set of rules—the law of lion and ox. The issue I have with such critics is epistemological and finally ethical, but to spell it out would require more space than is available here. I trust that my essay gives some indication of the issues, about which I shall speak in due course.

---

*February 1977.

The Absurdist Moment in Contemporary Literary Theory

Hayden White

Any attempt to characterize the present state of literary criticism must first deal with the fact that contemporary literary criticism does not constitute a coherent field of theory and practice.[1] The contours of criticism are unclear, its geography unspecified and its topography therefore uncertain. As a form of intellectual practice, no field is more imperialistic. Modern literary critics recognize no disciplinary barriers, either as to subject matter or to methods. In literary criticism, anything goes. This science of rules has no rules. It cannot even be said that it has a preferred object of study.

It might be thought *a priori* that literary criticism is distinguishable from other kinds of intellectual activity by virtue of its interest in the specifically literary artifact. But this is true only in a general sense. Modern literary critics resemble their historical prototypes by virtue of their interest in "literature" and their concentration on the "literary" artifact as the point of departure for the composition of their discourse. But this interest and this

---

[1] For bibliographical details on the anthologies cited in this essay, see Krieger's introduction. References in the body of the text refer to these editions. The only exceptions to this rule are two: Geoffrey H. Hartman, *The Fate of Reading and Other Essays* (Chicago: Univ. of Chicago Press, 1975), and Jacques Derrida, "White Mythology," *NLH*, 6, No. 1 (Autumn 1974), 5-74.

concentration are only *theoretical* possibilities for many modern critics—and this because modern criticism has no firm sense of what "literature" consists of or what a specifically "literary" artifact looks like. It does not know where to draw the line between "literature" on the one side and "language" on the other. It is not even sure that it is necessary, desirable, or even possible to draw that line.

For many—though by no means all or even a majority of—modern critics, since everything is potentially interpretable as language, then everything is potentially interpretable as literature; or, if language is regarded as merely a special case of the more comprehensive field of semiotics, nothing is interpretable as a specifically "literary" phenomenon, "literature" as such does not exist, and the principal task of *modern* literary criticism (if the point is taken to the end of the line) is to preside over its own dissolution. The position is manifestly Absurd; for the critics who hold this view, not only *continue to write* about the virtues of silence, they do so at interminable length and *alta voce*. In the thought of Bataille, Blanchot, Foucault, and Jacques Derrida, we witness the rise of a movement in literary criticism which raises the critical question only to take a grim satisfaction in the contemplation of the impossibility of ever resolving it or, at the extreme limit of thought, even of asking it. Literature is reduced to writing, writing to language, and language, in a final paroxysm of frustration, is reduced to chatter about silence. This apotheosis of "silence" is the inevitable destiny of a field of study which has slipped its cultural moorings; but the drift of literary criticism is not more random than that of Western culture in general. It is not only in literary criticism that babble ceases to be a problem in order to become a rule. But nowhere is this rule honored more than by those Absurdist critics who criticize endlessly in defense of the notion that criticism is impossible.

To be sure, most critics—what we should call Normal critics—continue to believe that literature not only *has* sense but *makes* sense of experience. Most critics continue to believe, accordingly, that criticism is both necessary and possible. Normal criticism is not a problem, then—at least, to Normal critics. *Their* problem is Absurdist criticism, which calls the practices of Normal criticism into doubt. It would be well, of course, for Normal critics to ignore their Absurdist critics, or rather their Absurdist *meta*critics—for Absurdist criticism is more about criticism than it is about literature. When the Absurdist critic—Foucault, Barthes, Derrida—comments on a literary artifact, it is always in the interest of making a *meta*critical point. But it is difficult for the Normal critic to ignore the Absurdist critic, for the latter always shows himself to take the critical enterprise more seriously than the former: he is willing to bring the critical enterprise itself under question. And how can a Normal critic deny the legitimacy of the impulse to criticize criticism? Once criticism is launched on its course of questioning, how can it halt before it has questioned itself?

But this is a domestic problem within criticism. Why should the cultural historian take Absurdist criticism seriously? What is the status of Absurdist criticism, considered as a datum of cultural history? Why should the cultural historian consider Absurdist criticism a privileged datum in any consideration of the condition of literary criticism in our time?

Unlike New Criticism, practical criticism, and formalism, even phenomenological criticism, the Absurdists do not represent a reform movement within the critical community. They do not take the critical activity for granted, and then go on to recommend specific methodological reforms that will permit it to do better what it had always done adequately. On the contrary, the Absurdists attack the whole critical enterprise, and they attack it where Normal criticism in all its forms is most vulnerable: language theory. For the older critical conventions language itself was not a problem. Language was simply the medium embodying the literary message. The purpose of criticism was to penetrate through the medium, by philological analysis, translation, grammatical and syntactical explication, in order to get at the message, the "meaning," the semantic level that lay beneath it. The interpretive problem arose once this deeper level had been reached. Absurdist criticism, by contrast, treats language itself as a problem and lingers indefinitely on the surface of the text, in the contemplation of language's power to hide or diffuse meaning, to resist decoding or translation, and ultimately to bewitch understanding by an infinite play of signs.

This is not to say that the Absurdist critics participate in the attempt of Chomsky and other technical linguists to create a science of language. On the contrary, their enterprise is completely different. They draw their inspiration from Nietzsche, Mallarmé, and Heidegger, all of whom treated language as the human problem par excellence, the disease which made "civilization" possible and generated its mutilating "discontents." But they dress up their attack on language with a terminology borrowed from Saussure, so as to give it a technical flavor and place conventional critics on the defensive at the point where they are most vulnerable, at the surface levels of the text, before what had normally been thought of as "interpretation" even begins. Precisely because Normal criticism had not viewed language itself as a problem (only a puzzle which had to be solved before moving to the real problem, the disclosure of the meaning hidden within language), it was vulnerable to a critical strategy which supposed that the problem of interpretation lay on the surface of discourse, in the very language in which the discourse at once revealed and concealed its own meaninglessness.

Absurdist criticism brings the status of the text, textuality itself, under question. In doing so, it locates a stress point of conventional criticism and exposes an unacknowledged assumption of all previous forms of criticism, the assumption of the transparency of the text, the assumption that, with enough learning and cleverness, the text can be seen through to the "meaning" (more or less ambiguous) that lies below its surface texture.

For the Absurdist critic, the notion of the text becomes an all-inclusive category of the interpretive enterprise; that or else the text is conceived to exist nowhere at all, to disappear in the flux of language, the play of signs. This fetishization of the text or of textuality is not, however, the product of an impulse that is alien to conventional criticism. There has always been a tendency in criticism to deify the text, to conceive the text as the very paradigm of experience, and to conceive the act of reading as a favored analogue of the way we make sense of everything. There has always been an impulse in criticism to view the text as, according to Hillis Miller, the Geneva School critic Beguin views it: as a sacrament that bears "precious witness . . . of God's presence in creation" ("The Geneva School," in Simon, p. 289).

But what is the status of the text in a culture that no longer believes in God, in tradition, in culture, civilization, or even "literature"? It then becomes possible to treat the text as either a signifier that is its own signified (Derrida) or as a mere " 'collection of signs given without relation to ideas, language, or style, and intended to define within the density of all modes of possible expression the solitude of ritual language' " (Barthes, quoted by Velan, in Simon, p. 332). This is especially the case with the structuralist approach to the text. As Edward W. Said says, for the structuralist, "Everything is a text . . . or . . . nothing is a text" ("*Abecedarium Culturae:* Structuralism, Absence, Writing" in Simon, p. 379). The text thus becomes either an analogue of Being or its antithesis. In either case, with such views at the top of the list of enabling postulates of criticism, it is easy to understand how "the act of reading" could become fetishized, turned into a mystery which is at once a fascinating and at the same time cruelly mutilating activity. And it is understandable how, given the notion of the text as "everything . . . or . . . nothing," criticism would be driven to try to distinguish rigidly between what might be called "master readers" and "slave readers," that is to say, readers endowed with the authority to dilate on the mysteries of the texts and readers lacking that authority. Not surprisingly, then, much of contemporary criticism turns on the effort to establish the criteria for determining the techniques and the authority of the privileged reader.

This fascination with the notion of the privileged reader is itself symptomatic of the Absurdist possibility contained within the general field of literary criticism in a post-industrial society. It reflects a general want of confidence in our ability to locate reality or the centers of power in post-industrial society and to comprehend them when they are located. In a society in which both structures and processes are indeterminable, all activities become questionable, even criticism, even reading. But because these activities continue to be practiced, continue to claim authority without adequate theoretical grounds for that claim, it becomes imperative to determine who is responsible for them and why they should be practiced at all. Reading becomes as problematical as writing, politics, or business, and like them, the perquisite of the privileged few.

Of course, reading had always been regarded as a precious human endowment, a luxury item, the sign as well as the basis of civilization, and the perquisite of the few. But it was also traditionally regarded as a talent which all men in principle possessed, was seen therefore as an ordinary human activity, requiring only normal human talents for its acquisition. But under the imperative to mystify the text, itself a function of a prior imperative to mystify language, reading takes on magical qualities, is seen as a privilege of a few exceptional intelligences. It is not surprising, therefore, that some of the more Absurdist of modern critics view "reading" as well as "writing" as "dangerous" activities, to be entered into only under the most carefully regulated conditions or under the direction of those professional readers who make up the elite of the critical community.

Thus, for example, Heidegger defines language as man's most dangerous possession ("Hölderlin and the Essence of Poetry," in Gras, p. 31), while Jean Paulhan conceives language as "betrayal" (Alvin Eustis, "The Paradoxes of Language: Jean Paulhan," in Simon, p. 110). According to Beaujour, Bataille views literature as the paradigm of "transgression" ("Eros and Nonsense: Georges Bataille," in Simon, p. 149), while Maurice Blanchot, as de Man tells us, conceives the "reading process" to be located "before or beyond the act of understanding" ("Maurice Blanchot," in Simon, p. 257). And Said writes that Derrida believes that writing "partici-pates constantly in the violence of each trace it makes" ("*Abecedarium Culturae*," in Simon, p. 385). Mystification of the text results in the fetishism of writing and the narcissism of the reader. The privileged reader looks everywhere and finds only texts, and within the texts only himself.

This is by no means an attitude found only in the Absurdist critics whom Eustis calls the "Terrorists" ("The Paradoxes of Language," in Simon, pp. 111-12). It was potentially present in the very activity of criticism from the beginning. Consider a less extreme example. Georges Poulet can hardly be regarded as a Terrorist. In his critical practice he is much closer to such con-ventional critical schools as those represented by the New Critics in America, the practical critics of Great Britain, and the history-of-ideas tradition represented by the late A. O. Lovejoy, or the philological tradition of Spitzer—the old guard of contemporary criticism. Yet in a remarkable celebration of his own reading experience as a paradigm of critical practice, Poulet, in the famous essay on the "Phenomenology of Reading," ends by saying:

It seems then that criticism, in order to accompany the mind in this effort of detachment from itself, needs to annihilate, or at least momentarily to forget, the objective elements of the work, and to elevate itself to the apprehension of a subjectivity without objectivity. (in Polletta, p. 118)

The naive reader must ask, What can this mean? What could a "subjectivity without objectivity" consist of? Poulet continues to believe in the reality of the literary work and to view it as the product of a recognizable human activity. "There is," he writes, "in the [literary] work a mental activity profoundly engaged in objective forms. . . ." At the same time, however, he postulates "another level" of the work where, "forsaking all forms, a subject . . . reveals itself to itself (and to me) in its transcendence over all which is reflected in it." When the reader, or rather Poulet (for he is a solitary reader) reaches this point, "no object can any longer express it, no structure can any longer define it; it is exposed in its ineffability and its fundamental indeterminacy" (*ibid.*).

As thus characterized, the literary text has all the attributes of godhead, spirit, or numen; it is an effect which is its own cause and a cause which is its own effect. This is precisely the point of view of the Terrorist, Blanchot, who insists, with Mallarmé, that the book "comes into being by itself; it is made, and exists, by itself" (de Man, in Simon, p. 263). But unlike Blanchot, who insists that not even the author can read his own work (*ibid.*, p. 260), Poulet suggests that the work reads itself through him. As he puts it:

I ought not to hesitate to recognize that so long as it is animated by this vital inbreathing inspired by the act of reading, a work of literature becomes (at the expense of the reader whose own life it suspends) a sort of human being, that it is a mind conscious of itself and constituting itself in me as the subject of its own objects.

The work lives its own life within me; in a certain sense, it thinks itself, and it even gives itself a meaning within me. ("Phenomenology of Reading," in Polletta, p. 109)

What could be more Orphic! It is not a matter of taking this passage as a figurative approximation to what Poulet literally experiences in the act of reading. When we speak theoretically, we are as responsible for the figures of speech that we use to limn a problem as we are for the words we choose to denote its content. Here the work is personified in the mode of spirit, the act of reading becomes constitutive of meaning, and the exchange between work and reader is construed in the manner of an invasion of consciousness by a ghostly (though always benign) presence. It is not surprising that Poulet uses the language of schizophrenic analysis to gloss this idea:

A lag takes place, a sort of schizoid distinction between what I feel and what the other feels; a confused awareness of delay, so that the work seems first to think by itself, and then to inform me what it has thought. Thus I often have the impression, while reading, of simply witnessing an action which at the same time concerns and yet does not concern me. This provokes a certain feeling of surprise within me. I am a consciousness astonished by an existence which is not mine, but which I experience as though it were mine.

This astonished consciousness is in fact the consciousness of the critic. . . . (*ibid.*, p. 110)

What is astonishing about Poulet's identification of astonishment with the critical consciousness is that he refuses to remain struck dumb, stunned, but rather writes incessantly about his own astonishment before (or within) the text. In this respect he differs not at all from the Absurdist critic who denies the possibility of criticism altogether, and does so over and over again in a celebration of a capacity to misunderstand, which, in the excessive length in which it is elaborated, denies its own authenticity. This is all the more interesting in that Poulet's celebration of reading as an Orphic initiation rite is advanced in the interest of defending "literature" against its assimilation to mere writing, on the one side, and to the realm of merely material artifacts, on the other. But the effect on the conceptualization of the nature of reading and the tasks of criticism is the same. Poulet makes of reading a sacrament and of criticism the discipline of disciplines, as theology was (or claimed to be) in the Middle Ages, though as a discipline the most it aspires to is, not understanding, only "astonishment."

How can we account for the tendency, manifested by a number of the critics of our time, to mystify "literature" and to turn "reading" into a mystery in which only the most deeply initiated may authoritatively participate? In *The Fate of Reading*, Geoffrey Hartman finds the cause of the current critical babble in "a new *mal du siècle*." Words lose their value, along with all other "signs," because they have been overproduced through the "stimulus-flooding" of the media. We "know" too much; or rather we have too much "information." And the result is "restlessness: . . . We seem unable to close off a subject, or any inquiry. Closure is death" (Hartman, pp. 250-51). The disappearance of literature into language and of language into signs inevitably inflates the value of the critical performance while at the same time investing that performance with the aspect of a mystery. The critic no longer knows exactly why he is doing what he does or how he does it; yet he cannot stop. He is in the grip of a *vis interpretativa*, the compulsive power of which impels the critic to reflect more on criticism than on "reading." Metacriticism becomes the mode. "Literature is today so easily assimilated or coopted that the function of criticism must often be to defamiliarize it." So Hartman writes. The same can be said of criticism itself. In this situation the critic is tempted to defamiliarize criticism. And one of the ways we can defamiliarize criticism is to claim for it the same authority that earlier critics claimed for "literature" only. Hartman, overcautiously, entertains the possibility that criticism is itself "an art form," but seems unwilling to draw the implications of that view. He takes refuge, instead, behind the contention that "reading" must be restored as "that conscious and scrupulous form of it we call literary criticism" (*ibid.*, p. 272).

Hartman's distress can be viewed as a symptom of the *mal du siècle* which he seeks to transcend. The message of the Absurdist critics is clear: in a society in which human labor itself has ceased to be either a value or that which confers value on its products, neither literary texts nor anything else can claim an ontologically privileged status. Literary texts are commodities, just like all the other entities inhabiting the realm of culture, differing from natural objects solely by virtue of the amount of money they can claim in an exchange or market economy. And as long as the value of human labor remains unrecognized or undetermined, or construed in terms of its exchange value for a money equivalent, the artistic artifact will remain subject to the kind of fetishization to which money itself is subject. The effort on the part of Poulet, and of Hartman, to restore dignity to the act of reading will continue to be subject to the tendency to mystification as long as all other specifically human forms of labor remain devalued, undervalued, or valued solely in terms of money.

It is hardly surprising that criticism is in crisis. Since it is, after all, quintessentially a valuative activity, it is subject to the mysteries of valuation which prevail in the determining sector of modern social life: the economic. Inevitably, critics—professional readers of texts—have a stake in inflating the value both of their own activity and of the objects, texts, which are the occasion of that activity. One of the ways to effect this inflation is to endow the literary work with all the attributes of a "spirit" whose disappearance in the wake of a profound materialization of culture is signalled only by those "vapor trails" which Nietzsche espied on the receding horizon of "civilization." This is the path taken by

Poulet and other representatives of Normal criticism from the New and practical critics of the interwar years through the archetypal criticism of Northrop Frye and the representatives of the Yale School in our own time.

Another way to inflate the value of both literature and criticism is that taken by the line of critics from Heidegger and the early Sartre through phenomenology and structuralism. This way stresses the "demonic" nature of literature, language, and culture in general. This process of demonization prepares the way for the reception of the Absurdist discourse of Bataille, Blanchot, and others, and culminates in Barthes, Foucault, and Derrida. By denying the privileged status of literature and the literary artifact, the Absurdist critics simply push the impulse to commodify everything to its logical—and absurd—conclusion.

Thus, when Foucault says that "words" or "language" are simply "things" among the other things that inhabit the world, he is less interested in ontologically demoting words and language than in challenging those cultural conventions which set "culture" over against "nature" in the mode of qualitative opposition, identifying "culture" with "spirit," and "nature" with "matter" in theory but in practice treating every cultural artifact as nothing but "commodity." Foucault is less interested in despiritualizing "culture" than in renaturalizing it; or rather simply naturalizing it, since in his view, "culture" has been laboring under the delusion of its "spirituality" since the foundation of society. It is this interest in the despiritualization of the cultural artifacts of modern society which links him and Barthes with the grandiose, anticivilizational project of Lévi-Strauss. Like Lévi-Strauss, Foucault and Barthes see the function of criticism as the demythologization of the myths of modern industrial society. To demythologize, Barthes insists, is to show how every cultural artifact laying claim to the status of the "natural" is in reality "artificial" and, in the end, nothing but a human product. To reveal the human origin of those ideas and practices which society takes as "natural," is to show how "unnatural" they are and is to point attention to a genuinely human social order in which the quest for "spirituality" will have been laid definitively to rest because "culture" will be regarded as continuous with, rather than disjoined from, nature.

It is within the context of this larger, socially utopian enterprise that the Absurdist attitudes toward criticism as an activity and toward other, Normal, critics are to be understood. For the

Absurdist, criticism's role is to take the side of "nature" against "culture." Whence the celebration by these critics of such anti-social phenomena as barbarism, criminality, insanity, childishness, anything that is violent and irrational in general. The dark side of civilized existence, that which, as Nietzsche said, had to be given up or repressed or confined or simply ignored, if civilization was to have been founded in the first place, has simply been avoided by the Normal critics who define their principal task as the defense of civilization against all of these things. So, too, insofar as Normal criticism takes "literature" or "art" to consist only of those creations of man which reinforce his capacities for repression, bad faith, or genteel violence, it must be seen as complicit in the very processes of self-denial that characterize modern consumptive societies.

Absurdist criticism achieves its critical distance on modern culture, art, and literature by reversing the hitherto unquestioned assumption that "civilization" is worth the price paid in human suffering, anxiety, and pain by the "uncivilized" of the world (primitive peoples, traditional cultures, women, children, the outcasts or pariahs of world history) and asserting the rights of the "uncivilized" against the "civilizers." Absurdist criticism is informed by the intuition that "art" and "literature" are not innocent activities which, even in their best representatives, are totally without complicity in the exploitation of the "many" by the "few." On the contrary, by their very nature as social products, art and literature are not only complicit in the violence which sustains a given form of society, they even have their own dark underside and origin in criminality, barbarism, and will-to-destruction.

Art and literature, in the Absurdist estimation, cannot only heal but also wound, cannot only unite but divide, cannot only elevate but debase—and in fact continually do so in the interest of those who possess the power and privilege of dominant classes in all societies known to history. This is why the Marquis de Sade is the presiding presence of the criticism which develops under the aspect of Absurdist attacks on literature, art, civilization, and humanity itself. Sade, Marx, Nietzsche, and Freud are the four sages of this critical tradition because they taught, in one way or another, what Dostoyevsky put into words that have become the sanctioning cliché of so many modern cultural movements: if God is dead, everything is permitted. To find out what are the limits of the freedom that this cliché licenses is the principal aim of Absurdist criticism.

Absurdist criticism, then, is programmatically "abnormal." It brings the very concepts of the normal and the normative in modern society under question. And it does so by insisting on the abnormality of those values which Normal criticism takes for granted. Normal criticism seeks to ignore or dismiss this charge against *it* of being abnormal, but it cannot do so consistently. First, because Absurdist criticism continues to grow among younger critics who remain fascinated by the boldness of its enabling postulates; but second and more important, Absurdist criticism is merely a logical extension of dominant but unacknowledged principles that have resided at the heart of Normal criticism itself since its crystallization in the period before and after World War II.

It must be asked, then: What is Normal criticism? Negatively, it is anything that is not Absurdist; but positively it can be defined by certain recognizable attributes. First, Normal criticism takes shape against the background of the various forms of criticism practiced in the universities prior to World War II. These forms of criticism were various but they were all essentially normative in their practice. And although displaying various degrees of theoretical consciousness, they were not characterized by a very high degree of theoretical self-consciousness. That is to say, although they brought different theories to bear upon the literary artifact, in order to interpret it, disclose its meanings, locate it in its several historical contexts, and so on, they did not take criticism itself to be a problem. On the contrary, they tended to take the existence of literary criticism as a datum, as a fact of life, as it were, and moved directly from the question "Why criticize?" to the theoretically posterior problem of "How criticize?" The criticism which prevailed in the universities during the interwar years may have been inspired by various general notions of the tasks of criticism, inspired by philosophers as different as Arnold, Croce, Taine, or Dilthey, but these notions were entertained "naively" insofar as they were assumed justifications for criticizing rather than treated as grounds for problematic consideration of the nature of criticism in general.

We may call this mode of critical address *Elementary* in the sense that it did not question the possibility of the critic's service to literature, his ability to plumb the depths of meaning of a text, of situating a text within its historical contexts, and of communicating the features of the text's structure and content to the common reader. Literature as thus conceived was "precious," but it was not mysterious; it was taken to serve unambiguously the causes of such higher values as culture, civilization, humanity, or life; the critic's purpose was to distinguish "good" from "bad" or "flawed" literature and then go on to demonstrate how the "good" literature did well what the "bad" literature did imperfectly.

But over against this Elementary mode of criticism there arose in the interwar years an alternative mode whose center of activity was outside the university (or only peripherally within it). This other mode threatened both the concept of literature and the notions of the critic's task which the Elementary mode shared with its nineteenth-century progenitors. This new mode was represented by Marxism, psychoanalysis, and the various forms of the sociology of knowledge spawned by the age of ideology. It was a characteristic of all of these anti-academic schools of criticism to challenge the "innocence" of culture in general, to view literature as an epiphenomenon of more basic, human or social drives and needs, and to define the task of criticism as the unmasking of the ideological understructure of the text and the disclosure of the ways in which not only literature, but all forms of art, sublimated, obscured, or reinforced human impulses more or less "physical" or more or less "social" in nature, but in any event specifically pre-aesthetic and pre-moral. These critical conventions were thus *Reductive* in nature, conceiving the aim of the critic, not as the union with the artwork in the mode of empathy, *nacherleben*, or celebration, but rather as the achievement of distance on the artwork, its torturing, and the revelation of its hidden, more basic, and preliterary content.

But none of the representatives of these conventions—neither Lukács, Trotsky, Brecht, Hauser, Mannheim, Caudwell, Benjamin, Adorno, Freud, Reich, or the other psychoanalysts—were enemies of literature or criticism. They all shared a common faith in the possibility of a favored "method" for mediating between the human content of the artwork they analyzed and the human needs of those who read them. Moreover, they all shared a belief in the possibility of communication with, and translations between, different communities of critics. They might disclose as the true content of a given artwork the operations of the social relations of

production, the psyche, or the ideology informing the consciousness of its creator, thereby "reducing" the specifically aesthetic
aspects of the artwork to the status of manifestation of more basic
drives, needs, or desires. But they viewed such drives, needs, and
desires as universally human products of the social condition of
mankind, on the basis of a knowledge of which they could assess
and rank artworks as being "progressive" or "retrogressive." And
they conceived it as the function of the critic to promote the
cause of the progressive forces in human life, in much the same
way that Arnold had done—even though their conception of what
was culturally "healthy," and what was not, differed from his *toto
caelo*.

The Reductivist mode of criticism arose concomitantly with
the overt politicization of criticism which the totalitarian regimes
of Russia, Germany, and Italy promoted during the interwar years.
And the immediate enemies of liberal and radical practitioners of
Reductivism were the intellectual and artistic "lackeys" of these
totalitarian regimes rather than the academics who practiced criticism in the Elementary mode. What they opposed principally was
the "false reductionism" of Fascist critics, writers, and intellectu-
als. But because they tended to view academic criticism as being
at least tacitly allied with Fascism, by virtue, if nothing else, of its
failure to perceive the ideological implications of a generally
"ethical" or openly "aestheticist" criticism, they attacked academic
criticism as well.

It is in the light of this attack by the Reductivists on the
criticism that prevailed in the academy that the theoretical movements of New Criticism, practical criticism, and to a certain extent
formalism, the schools which moved to the forefront of academic
criticism during and after World War II, can be understood. These
schools sought to provide a theoretical basis for the critical practices of the academy in ways that would counter the Reductivists'
charge that such practices were, when not nefarious, at least
theoretically naive. Each of these schools of criticism sought to
gain a theoretical distance on the artwork in a way like that of
Marxists, psychoanalysts, and sociologists of knowledge, but so as
not to threaten what traditional humanistic thought conceived to
be the specifically "aesthetic" aspect of the "artwork."

New Criticism, practical criticism, and formalism concen-
trated on the aesthetic, moral, and epistemological significance of
the literary artwork respectively, but in what was intended to be a

nonreductive way, that is to say, in such a way as to leave the "literariness" of "literature" unquestioned. Unlike the older academic criticism represented by, say, Spitzer and the philological school, which sought to place the critic "in the creative center of the artist . . . and to recreate the artistic organism," the New Critics, practical critics, and formalists tried to keep the artwork at a distance from the critic (and the reader) so that its integrity as art could be made manifest. But the integrity of the work as art consisted, for all of these critical conventions, in the extent to which the work stood over against or in contrast to "life."

Practical critics such as Trilling and Leavis might construe the critic's task as that of "bearing personal testimony" to the aesthetic and moral values contained in the works being studied, but these values were worthy of "testimony" only insofar as they represented a transcendence of, or alternative to, the values of ordinary human existence. The New Critics might insist that the task of the critic was to show what the work "did" rather than what it "meant," but this was because artworks "did" things that no other cultural artifact (and very few human beings) could ever do. Formalist critics might urge their colleagues to undertake the redescription of the artwork in such a way as to show its generic similarities to other artworks within a given tradition or even to disclose the popular or folk artforms that gave them their distinctive attributes and persuasive power. But this suggested that the literary world was self-contained and self-generating, hovered above other departments of culture and bore little responsiblity to them, and finally existed for itself alone—like a Platonic idea or an Aristotelian autotelic form. Criticism in this mode may thus be called *Inflationary*, differing as it did from the Elementary mode by virtue of its theoretical self-consciousness, and from the Reductivist mode by its desire to save the sphere of art from a theoretical grounding in "mere" life.

By the end of World War II, then, the critical scene can be viewed as having been colonized by representatives of three distinctive critical modes: the Elementary, the Reductive, and the Inflationary. All three modes were elaborated under the assumption of the service that the critic could render to "literature" and the benefits that "literature" could confer on "civilization." But the kind of service which criticism could render to literature and the methods to be used in the rendering of that service were differently construed. Representatives of the Elementary mode simply took the existence of "literature" for granted, defined it by its difference from the quotidian elements of culture, and then went on to assume that this literary realm could be penetrated by the critic and, ultimately, grounded in the "history" of the culture out of which it had originally arisen.

Against the "naiveté" of the Elementary mode, the Reductivist critics mounted an attack, not only against the traditional humanistic distinction between "literature" and "life," but also against the conception of humanistic study on which Elementary criticism was based. The Reductivists grounded literature in life with a vengeance. For them, literature was not the antithesis of life, but a sublimation of forces more basic, forces that gave to human life its various forms. The critic's task, as the Reductivists saw it, was to analyze literary works "scientifically" and to determine the liberating (progressive) or repressive (reactionary) content of specific works.

To the Elementary critics, this Reductivist mode constituted a threat to literature every bit as dangerous as the kind of criticism promoted by the totalitarian regimes against which the Reductivists had raised up their challenge. But Elementary criticism could not defend itself against the Reductivists, because it was congenitally suspicious of all forms of metatheoretical speculation. It was left to the Inflationary critics—represented by the New, practical, and formalist theorists—to defend "literature" against reductivism in all its forms.

The Inflationary critics shared a common desire to place literary study and criticism on an "objective" basis. Instead of the impressionistic methods that had prevailed in the Elementary mode and the pseudo-scientistic methods used in the Reductivist mode, the methods of the Inflationary critics were to be "objective." To be objective, however, meant to treat the artwork as a thing-in-itself, a specifically aesthetic artifact, linked in a number of different ways to its various historical contexts but ultimately governed by its own autotelic principles. The extreme manifestation of the Inflationary attitude was that which took shape in the New Critics' efforts to defend their claims of autotelism for the artwork. They progressively sheared away, as interpretatively trivial, the relations which the literary artifact bore to its historical context, its author, and its audience(s), leaving the ideal critical situation to be conceived as that in which a single sensitive reader, which usually turned out to be a New Critic, studied a single literary work in the effort to determine the inner dynamics of the work's intrinsic irony.

Formalism located the individual work within a given generic tradition, but insisted, as Northrop Frye was later to insist in his *Anatomy of Criticism*, the *locus classicus* of archetypal criticism, that all literature was either about other literature or about the religious myths that historically preceded and informed every discernible literary tradition. Practical criticism was more historically responsible, it could be argued, in that it at least set the moral over against the purely aesthetic impulse as the occasion of all culturally significant art. But insofar as practical criticism tended toward the identification of "significant art" with the "Great Tradition" of Western European literary practice, it remained subject to the attack on its elitism and parochialism which Marxism, psychoanalysis, and sociology of knowledge had brought to bear upon the conventional criticism of its academic predecessors.

The Inflationary mode of criticism was an extension of many of the principles that had informed the Elementary mode, but went further in its efforts to insulate "literature" from "life" and "art" from the "historical process" in which it arose. Old-fashioned philological criticism at least linked up literature with language and cultural forms, and imagined a relationship between the artwork and the milieus in which the literary work was written and subsequently read. Inflationary criticism, by contrast, insisted on the isolation of the sphere of literature (if not *from* "life") at least *within* the "tradition" of high culture which floated above and ultimately gave meaning to the lives of civilizations.

It would not do to say, without qualification, that the Inflationary mode fetishized the artwork and turned criticism into a priestly service to the object thus fetishized. But for the critics who worked within this mode, the basis for such fetishism was potentially present. Their tendency to locate literature within a realm of cultural being which hovered above and gave meaning to "ordinary human existence" but which was governed by its own autotelic principles did tend to make of literature a mystery which only the most sensitive initiate into the "tradition" that provided its context could unravel. Moreover, there was inherent in the Inflationary mode from the beginning a purely contemplative impulse which denied implicitly the claims to objectivity which they made for their critical practice. Whatever literature was, whether it was the single work, the tradition within which the work had its being, or the genre of which it was a species-type, it was still something ultimately "other" than mere life. In this tendency to endow "art" with a value which mere life itself could never lay claim to, the Inflationary critics seemed to be saying that if a choice between them had to be made, they would choose art over life every time.

It was the inflation of art at the expense of life that drew the ire of the existentialist critics of the war period. Fed up with ideology in all its forms, they regarded the pervasive formalism of the Inflationary mode as unresponsive to the human needs and desires which inspired artistic creativity in the first place. In this objection, they resembled the practitioners of criticism in the Reductive mode; and this accounts for the tendency of many early existentialists to ally themselves with Marxists, psychoanalysts, and sociologists of knowledge. But they—or at least Sartre, Camus, and their followers—were equally fearful of the Reductivist tendencies of these anti-academic schools of criticism. And they insisted on opening up once more the basic questions which all literary theorists, including the Marxists, psychoanalysts, etc., had begged or simply not asked, such questions as "Why write?", "Why read?" and "Why criticize?"

Thus, in Sartre's work, the distinction between writing and criticizing is hardly made; the one activity is indistinguishable from the other. Both writing and criticizing are conceived as ways of closing the gap not only between literature and life, but also between art and work, thought and action, history and consciousness. Criticism, like writing in general, was viewed as action, not contemplation, as violent not pacific, as aggression not generosity —although Sartre, like Camus, desired that it would not be all these things. In any event, under the press of the existentialist critique of society as hell and culture as purgatory, the status of both literature and criticism were brought under radical doubt. And the emergence of both phenomenology and structuralism can be understood as post-existentialist types of critical practice intended to carry the radical doubt of existentialism to the end of the line, and to see whether it was justified or not.

This radical doubt is not, however, a merely literary or literary-critical doubt; it is an ontological and epistemological doubt, which finds expression in the phenomenological impulse to "bracket" the experience of any given consciousness in order to arrive at a notion of consciousness-in-general. In this effort, the activity of reading enjoys a favored place as a model of consciousness' activity as it confronts an alien world and tries to make sense of it.

Vernon Gras points out in his introduction to his anthology that if existentialism exists at all today, it must be understood as a "moment" in the evolution of the two critical schools which claim to provide solutions to the problematic which it elaborates: phenomenology and structuralism. These two movements, considered as frameworks for specific schools or conventions of literary criticism, share a tendency to elevate human consciousness into the fundamental category of Being-in-general (whence their fascination, not only with Hegel, but also with Heidegger) and to construe literature as a special case of that "language" which is consciousness' privileged instrument for conferring meaning on a world that inherently lacks it. This elevation of consciousness to the status of fundamental category of Being, combined with the notion that language in general represents the fundamental clue to the nature of consciousness, accounts for the tendency of phenomenologists and structuralists to elevate criticism into a high form of art, equal if not superior to poetry, on the one side, and to demote "literature" to a status lower than that of "language-in-general" on the other.

The consummation of the phenomenological-structuralist program we can designate as the *Generalized* mode of criticism, "generalized" insofar as all phenomena are not gathered under a single class of phenomena and thereby "reduced" to manifestations of the favored set, but rather placed on the same ontological level as manifestations of the mysterious human power to consign meaning to things through language. This human power to consign meaning is mysterious insofar as it is conceived to precede, logically if not ontologically, all of the efforts of the thinking, feeling, and willing subject to determine the meaning of meaning, or the status of meaning in the world. Language or speech is mysteriously invested with the power to create meanings and, at the same time, frustrate every effort to arrive at definitive meaning. As thus envisaged, literary expression can claim no privileged status in the universe of speech acts; it is merely one kind of speech act among the many which make up the human capacity to create, manipulate, and consume *signs*. But if literary expression can claim no special status, criticism considered as a science of semiology not only can, but does, lay claim to the status of science of sciences or art of arts. For semiology is the study of the paradoxical fact that in the very investment of things with meanings, humanity obscures from itself its own possible single meaning.

Some structuralists, especially Lévi-Strauss and his followers, claim to be involved in the search for a universal science of humanity, culture, or mind. But in reality they deny the possibility of a universal science of humanity, culture, or mind by the single-mindedness with which they insist on the uniqueness of all the forms of meaning which men, in their historical careers, confer on the world they inhabit. They appear, again paradoxically, to take delight in revealing that the science of the human, which they profess to aspire to, is actually impossible, due to the nature of the preferred object of that science, i.e., language, and to the nature of the technique alone capable of analyzing that object, *bricolage*, which is less interested in coherency and logical consistency (the attributes of any science known to history) than improvisation and attention to the function of the phenomenon in its specific spatio-temporal-cultural locale.

Such paradoxes as these point to a fundamental ambiguity in the enabling postulates of "the structuralist activity." This ambiguity arises from the simultaneous impulse to claim the authority of that positivistic scientific convention which is the secret enemy of most structuralists' activity, while claiming for the structuralists themselves the status of privileged interpreters of what humanity, culture, history, and civilization, not to mention literature, art, and language, are all about. This twofold and self-contradictory claim of the structuralists periodically erupts into impulses toward self-denial, manifested in the tendency to deny that there is any such thing as a structuralist philosophy or movement, on the one side, and in the desire to deny the value of science, culture, civilization, and even "humanity" itself (as in Foucault), on the other.

As thus envisaged, structuralism can be seen as what Northrop Frye would call an "existential projection" of the theory of the bifurcated nature of reality residing in the original Saussurian definition of speech as an opposition of *langue* to *parole*. Whatever the value of this definition for technical linguists, this definition of speech, when translated into a general theory of culture (as in Lévi-Strauss), of literature (as in Jakobson), of mind (as in Lacan), ideas (as in Foucault), or of signs (as in Barthes), can only generate irresolvable theoretical contradictions. These contradictions have been spelled out by Jacques Derrida, the current magus of the Parisian intellectual scene, who defines his aim as wishing to put himself "at a point so that I do not know any longer where I am going" ("Structure, Sign, and Play in the Discourse of the Human Sciences," in Macksey and Donato, p. 267). But this "I" which no longer knows where "it" is going is an important indicator of where this mode of criticism seeks to go. It signals the hypostatization of the critical "I," the dissociation of the critic from any collective human enterprise, the elevation of criticism to the status of the superscience that is at once purely subjective *and* willing to lay claim to universal significance. It is no accident that Nietzsche is invoked as the paradigm of this critical program; he is the archetype of a critical posture which celebrates solipsism as stance and will to power as method.

It is within the context of ideas such as these that we can comprehend the historical significance of the Absurdist moment in contemporary literary criticism. Structuralism "generalizes" the realm of literary texts, thereby tacitly affirming their shared value, but locates this value in their most obviously shared attribute, their status as linguistic artifacts. This is neither a reduction nor an inflation because the literary text is taken as precisely what it appears to be, i.e., a system of signs. In fact, rather than seeing the literary text as an epiphenomenon or manifestation of some more basic level of human consciousness or process, structuralism extends the notion of text to encompass *all* sign systems, from religious rituals to sport, eating habits, fashion, burial practices, economic behavior, and everything else. All cultural phenomena are seen as instances of the human capacity to produce, exchange, and consume signs. Accordingly, the interpretation of cultural phenomena is regarded as merely a special case of the act of reading in which the manipulation and exchange of signs is carried out most self-consciously, the act of reading *literary* texts.

Instead of regarding the literary text as a product of cultural processes more basic than writing, writing is taken as the crucial analogue of all those acts of signification by which meaning is conferred upon an otherwise meaningless existence, whence the pervasive melancholy of the structuralist activity; all of its "tropiques" are "tristes," because it perceives all cultural systems as products of the imposition of a purely fictive meaning on an otherwise meaningless reality. All meaning derives from language's power to bewitch intelligence with the promise of a meaning that can always be shown on analysis to be arbitrary and, ultimately, spurious. Books always disappoint us, structuralists believe, because their fictiveness always shines through to the critical intelligence capable of discerning their status as only a system of signs. And everything else in culture disappoints us too, as it is analyzed and disclosed to be nothing but a system of signs. How can any given system of signs—such as literature—claim any special value if every-thing, even "nature" ultimately, is effectively nothing but a system of signs? The structuralist cannot answer this question, because his answer would itself be nothing but a system of signs—hence as arbitrary as the experience of culture which had inspired the question in the first place.

At the heart of structuralism, then, resides an awareness of the arbitrary nature of the whole cultural enterprise and, *a fortiori*, of the critical enterprise. Absurdist criticism, which originally arose in the thought of Paulhan, Bataille, Blanchot, and Heidegger pri-marily as a sickness unto death with language, seizes upon this notion of arbitrariness and, in the thought of Foucault, Barthes, and Derrida, takes it to its logical conclusion. These thinkers make of the arbitrariness of the sign a rule and of the "freeplay" of signification an ideal.

Listen to Derrida speaking about the fundamental problems of the history of metaphysics:

The event I called a rupture, the disruption I alluded to at the beginning of this paper, would presumably have come about when the structurality of structure had to begin to be thought, that is to say, repeated, and this is why I said that this disruption was repetition in all of the senses of this word. From then on it became necessary to think the law which governed, as it were, the desire for the center in the constitution of structure and the process of signification prescribing its displacements and its substitutions for this law of the central presence—but a central presence which was never itself, which has always already been transported outside itself in its surrogate. The surro-gate does not substitute itself for anything which has somehow pre-existed it. From then on it was probably necessary to begin to think that there was no center, that the center could not be thought in the forms of a being-present, that the center had no natural locus, that it was not a fixed locus but a function, a sort of non-locus, in which an infinite number of sign-substitutions came into play. This moment was that in which language invaded the universal problematic; that in which, in the absence of a center or origin, everything became discourse—provided we can agree on this word—that is to say, when everything became a system where the central signified, the original or trans-cendental signified, is never absolutely present outside a system of differences. The absence of the transcendental signified extends the domain and the interplay or signification *ad infinitum*. ("Structure, Sign, and Play," in Macksey and Donato, p. 249)[2]

Derrida's philosophy—if it can be legitimately called that—represents nothing more than the hypostatization of the theory of discourse underlying and sanctioning the structuralist activity. He regards his own philosophy as a transcendence of the structuralist problematic, but he is wrong: it is its fetishization. He takes the Saussurian concept of speech as a dialectic of *langue* and *parole* and the Lévi-Straussian/Jakobsonian contrast between the metaphoric and metonymic poles of language use and treats them as the fundamental categories of Being. He may criticize Lévi-Strauss for his failure to demythologize his own thought; but Derrida is no less a mythologue when he reflects on the nature of what he calls "the interpretation of interpretation." Thus, for example, he writes that "there are . . . two interpretations of interpretation. . . . The one seeks to decipher, dreams of deciphering, a truth or an origin which is free from freeplay and from the order of the sign, and lives like an exile the necessity of interpretation. The other . . . affirms freeplay and tries to pass beyond man and humanism. . . . [and] does not seek in ethnography . . . the 'inspiration of a new humanism' . . ." (*ibid.*, pp. 264-65). As for himself, Derrida thinks there is no question of choosing between them, because,

in the first place . . . here we are in a region . . . where the category of choice seems particularly trivial; and in the second, because we must first try to conceive of the common ground, and the *différence* of this irreducible difference. Here there is a sort of question, call it historical, of which we are only glimpsing today the *conception, the formation, the gestation, the labor.* I employ these words, I admit, with a glance toward the business of childbearing—but also with a glance toward those who, in a company from which I do not exclude myself, turn their eyes away in the face of the as yet unnameable which is proclaiming itself and which can do so, as is necessary whenever a birth is in the offing, only under the species of the non-species, in the formless, mute, infant, and terrifying form of monstrosity. (*ibid.*, p. 265)

Here criticism becomes the celebration of an as yet unborn

---

[2] Quotations from Jacques Derrida, "Structure, Sign, and Play in the Discourse of the Human Sciences," in *The Languages of Criticism and the Sciences of Man: The Structuralist Controversy*, ed. Richard Macksey and Eugenio Donato, reprinted by permission of The Johns Hopkins University Press. Copyright © 1970 by The Johns Hopkins University Press.

and therefore unnameable "monstrosity." What could be more Absurdist? Not merely absurd, for the merely absurd is simply that which cannot be thought. Derrida not only thinks the unthinkable but turns it into an idol, his own equivalent of that *mana* which Lévi-Strauss defines as "at one and the same time force and action, quality and state, substantive and verb; abstract and concrete, omnipresent and localized.... it could almost be said that the function of notions like *mana* is to be opposed to the absence of signification, without entailing by itself any particular signification" (quoted by Derrida, in "Structure, Sign, and Play," in Macksey and Donato, pp. 261-62). Derrida sees himself as a critic of structuralism (see *ibid.*, p. 268), but as he characterizes his own point of view he is less the critic, than the victim, of that point of view. He is the minotaur imprisoned in structuralism's hypostatized labyrinth of language. As he himself admits:

Now I don't know what perception is and I don't believe that anything like perception exists. Perception is precisely a concept, a concept of an intuition or of a given originating from the thing itself, present itself in its meaning, independently from language, from the system of reference. And I believe that perception is interdependent with the concept of origin and of center and consequently whatever strikes at the metaphysics of which I have spoken strikes also at the very concept of perception. I don't believe that there is any perception. (*ibid.*, p. 272)

Here criticism is conceived literally to be blind; but instead of resenting this blindness, it takes delight in it and, like Oedipus, celebrates it as a sign of its authority to prophesy. On the surface, in Derrida, criticism has arrived, within the Absurdist moment at least, to the condition of pure farce in which it affirms its own "freeplay" on the one side and its "blindness" on the other.

Yet, there is a positive moment in the celebration of this carnival of criticism; it is literally a "lightening of the flesh," a "derealization" of the materialism of culture. In an essay entitled "White Mythology," intended to answer the question, "What is metaphysics?" (a Heideggerian question), Derrida suggests that the critical enterprise is linked up crucially with the problem of value in an exchange economy (*NLH*, 6, No. 1 [Autumn 1974], 16-17). He goes on to reduce the problem of exchange to the linguistic problem of the nature of metaphor.

Unlike Marx, however, whose discussion of the figurative basis of gold fetishism in the first chapter of *Capital* he cites, Derrida does not draw the conclusion that the escape from the fetishism of gold can be effected by the disclosure of the ways in which language itself bewitches the human power to see through the figurative to the literal meaning of "money-value." On the contrary, Derrida proceeds to show how any such "seeing through" is impossible, (*ibid.*, pp. 18 ff.). To see through the figurative to the literal meaning of any effort to seize experience in language is impossible, among other reasons, because there is no "perception" by which "reality" can be distinguished from its various linguistic figurations and the relative truth-content of competing figurations discerned (*ibid.*, pp. 44-46). There is *only figuration*, hence no privileged position from *within* language by which language can be called into question. Being, itself, is absurd. Therefore there is no "meaning," only the ghostly ballet of alternative "meanings" which various modes of figuration provide. We are indentured to an endless series of metaphorical translations from one universe of figuratively provided meaning to another. And they are all equally figurative.

But this disjunction of meaning from Being reveals the favored trope under which Derrida's own philosophizing (or anti-philosophizing) takes place. This trope is catachresis, the *ironic* trope par excellence. In his view, it is against the absurd imposition of meaning upon the meaningless that all of the other tropes (metaphor, metonymy, and synecdoche) arise. And it is against the absurd impulse to endow the meaningless with meaning that Derrida's own antiphilosophizing takes shape. Like the victims of "metaphor" whom he criticizes, however, Derrida reveals himself to be also a victim of a linguistic "turn." Instead of "existentially projecting" the tropes of metaphor, metonymy, and synecdoche onto Being, his favored trope, his trope of tropes, is catachresis (*abusio*). The "blind mouth" not only speaks, it speaks endlessly about its own "blindness." And we must ask, Is not this endless speech about blindness itself a projection of the elevation of *parole* over *langue*, a defense of speaking over both writing and listening?

Oracles are notoriously ambiguous. But oracularness is an unambiguous sign of a condition of culture, and, insofar as it gains favor within a given circle of intellectual work, an unambiguous sign of sterility. No wonder that the "monstrous" is celebrated and the "meaningless" deified. When work itself loses its meaning, why should intellectual work be exempted from drawing the consequences of its own mutilated condition?

We have come a far way, in too little time, from our original topic, which was the current condition of literary criticism. And our discourse has become infected by the sickness of those whose condition we wished to account for. One could easily dismiss the work of the Absurdist critics as merely another example of the mandarin culture in which it flourishes. They *are* absurd and their work is too precious to warrant the effort it takes to see through them to the cultural problems which their popularity reveals. But they are not incomprehensible; nor is their work insignificant.

The Absurdist critics represent a moment in the critical enterprise that was potentially present all along, present indeed from the time that Plato set the world of ideas over against the world of things and Aristotle set the contemplative life over against the active life as end to means. This Absurdist moment was potentially present from the beginning of modern European humanism, with its gnostic bent, its celebration of scholarship as an end in itself, its notion of privileged readers enjoying the status of priests interpreting the book of life to those who lived, worked, and died in "mere" life. It was potentially present in modern Western philosophy, with its insistence that things are never what they appear to be but are manifestations of noumenal essences whose reality must be supposed but whose "natures" can never be known. And it was present in modern, postromantic literary criticism, with its pretensions to objectivity, scientific accuracy, and privileged sensibility.

In Absurdist criticism, the dualism of Western thought and the elitism of Western social and cultural practice come home to roost. Now dualism is hypostatized as the condition of Being-in-general and meaninglessness is embraced as a goal. And elitism is stood on its head. When the world is denied all substance and perception is blind, who is to say who are the chosen and who the damned? On what grounds can we assert that the insane, the criminal, and the barbarian are wrong? And why should literature be accorded a privileged position among all the things created by man? Why should reading matter? And why should critics criticize with words when those who possess real power criticize with weapons? The Absurdist critics ask these questions, and in asking them, put the Normal critics in the position of having to provide answers which they themselves cannot imagine.

Differentiation and Undifferentiation in Lévi-Strauss and Current Critical Theory

René Girard

The conclusion of Claude Lévi-Strauss' *L'Homme nu*, entitled "Finale," asserts that myth embodies a principle of differentiation identical with language and thought.[1] Ritual, on the other hand, tries to retrieve an *undifferentiated immediacy*. Ritual tries to undo the work of language. Fortunately, Lévi-Strauss adds, this perverse undertaking will never succeed. The "undifferentiated" of ritual can only be made up of objects already differentiated by language and artifically pieced together.

Unlike "immediacy," about which we will speak later, the notion of "undifferentiated" certainly corresponds to part of what goes on in rituals all over the world: promiscuous sexual encounters, the overturning of hierarchies, the supposed metamorphosis of the participants into each other or into monstrous beings, etc. One cannot agree, however, that rituals are committed to this "undifferentiated" once and for all. All great traditional interpretations, notably the Hindu and the Chinese, attribute to ritual the end which Lévi-Strauss would reserve to myth alone: differentiation.

Before structuralism, no anthropologist had expressed a different view. Lévi-Strauss would reply that in all the examples that seem to verify my objection, language has been reintroduced and a secondary effect of differentiation has occurred, alien to ritual as such. Yet, there are innumerable instances of ritual differentiation visibly independent from the words that may or may not accompany them. In all *rites de passage*, for instance, the temporary loss of identity, or whatever ordeal the postulant may undergo, fits very well the undifferentiated conception of Lévi-Strauss but only

---

[1] *L'Homme nu* (1971) is the last volume of *Mythologiques* (Paris: Plon). The other volumes are *Le Cru et le cuit* (1964), *Du Miel aux cendres* (1966), *L'Origine des manières de table* (1968). Subsequent references to the "Finale" of *L'Homme nu* will be to this edition and will be indicated in the text in parentheses.

in a first phase which, rather than being an end in itself, is a means, paradoxical no doubt but constantly reasserted, toward the ultimate goal of ritual. This goal is obviously (re)differentiation since it consists in a new and stable status, a well-defined identity.

The same is true of sacrifice, singled out in *La Pensée sauvage* for a preliminary skirmish against ritual.[2] Frequently, the victim must be carved along rigorously defined lines which correspond to the structural subdivisions of the community. Each piece goes to its own subdivision. Here again, the first phase belongs to the undifferentiated which culminates in the immolation where it turns into its opposite. The communion aspect of sacrifice coincides not with the undifferentiated which is invariably conflictual but with the end result which is the regeneration of differences.

If ritual is no less committed to differentiation than myth, the converse is true: myth is no less involved with the undifferentiated than ritual. A cursory examination will reveal that it is the same involvement; it occurs in the same manner and probably for the same reasons. The undifferentiated presents itself as preliminary to (re)differentiation and often as its prerequisite. The original chaos of the Greeks, the *tohu wa bohu* of Genesis, Noah's flood, the ten plagues of Egypt, and the companions of Ulysses turned into swine by Circe are all examples of mythical undifferentiation.

In order to achieve this undifferentiation, myths, as well as rituals, resort to make-believe. They, too, piece back together entities which, "in reality," are already distinguished by language. Monsters are nothing else. We have a typical variation of this in a myth analyzed in *Le Cru et le cuit*. At the beginning, according to that myth, living creatures were so numerous and so compressed that they could not yet be distinguished. Later on, one single component is removed and the compactness of the mass is reduced. Interstices appear that make the necessary distinctions possible. Lévi-Strauss has a diagram showing that the space provided by the removal of even a small fragment can be distributed along a continuous line in such a way as to produce a number of separate segments, with no change in the total length of the figure. This myth and others are read by Lévi-Strauss not as differentiated solely, as any text would be, but as differentiation displaying itself. Myth is not simply structured, it is structuralist. It is not a mere

---

[2] Claude Lévi-Strauss, *La Pensée sauvage* (Paris: Plon, 1962), pp. 295-302.

product of symbolic thought, it is the process of symbolization made visible as process.

Lévi-Strauss also says that myths are able to think each other as myths. The formula has been most successful but its real meaning is not explained. It cannot mean only that many variations of the same myth are found. In nature, many varieties of the same species are found, many varieties of ants, for instance, but we would not say that these different ants think each other. In order for myths to think each other, it is necessary that each myth, up to a point, think itself as myth. And myths appear to think themselves because they provide the mirror in which they reflect their own process. Since the process is one of pure differentiation, the only appropriate mirror is the undifferentiated. This mirror is identical with the "primordial stuff" the myths are supposed to carve up. It is the presence in myths of the undifferentiated that allows Lévi-Strauss to say that they "think each other as myths."

In myth as well as in ritual, this undifferentiated can only be a *representation*. There is no difference and yet myth and ritual are treated quite differently by Lévi-Strauss. Ritual is severely rebuked for entertaining artificial representations of something language cannot really express. In myth, the same representations are praised, at least implicitly, since we would not even know without them that the myth intends to distinguish certain objects. We must have that first moment when these objects are supposed to be stuck together. In reality the undifferentiated plays the same role everywhere. Is it reasonable to describe the incentive for plunging a postulant into the undifferentiating waters of baptism as "a nostalgia for the immediate"? The postulant will not stay in there forever; he will drown only symbolically in order to reach the shore of a new differentiation.

The facts contradicting Lévi-Strauss are so massive that he cannot disregard them entirely. The combination of the undifferentiated plus differentiation is so commonplace that Lévi-Strauss grudgingly acknowledges its presence but he views it as no less unnatural and perverse than ritual. He explains it by the existence of bastardized myths that are primarily the account of some ritual. They should not influence our theoretical perception of the problem. The truth of the matter is that Lévi-Strauss is going to tortuous extremes of scholasticism to defend his assimilation of myth with differentiation and of ritual with the undifferentiated but it cannot be done. The two are always present together and their juxtaposition produces the standard profile of both myth and ritual. This profile has been identified and described in various languages and terminologies since time immemorial. To recognize this is to recognize a structural fact of life which Lévi-Strauss has always implicitly denied in his analyses and which he denies explicitly in the "Finale" of his *Mythologiques*. It must be possible to recognize that fact without compromising with the spiritualist exploitations of myth.

If the useful categories of the undifferentiated and differentiation are not manipulated in order to fit a preconceived formula, these categories help us understand the structural parallelism of myth and ritual. There are no anthropological reasons to cast myth as the hero and ritual as the villain in a drama of human intelligence. The reverse formula has already been tried, at least up to a point, with equally unsatisfactory results. The reasons for this anthropological Supreme Court are not anthropological. A major one, of course, is the structuralist commitment to the so-called "model" or "pilot" science of linguistics. Ritual uses language extensively but not exclusively like myth. This really leaves no choice. Since Lévi-Strauss is almost as eager to castigate religion as to extol language, he can assimilate the nonverbal means of ritual to the hard core of religious behavior and kill two ideological birds with the same stone.

There is still another bird from whose back Lévi-Strauss likes to pluck a few feathers once in a while, and it is philosophy. This third *bête noire* is also assimilated to ritual. The definition of ritual as "a nostalgia for the immediate" has a curiously philosophical ring for an anthropologist. One of the reasons could be that it is also Lévi-Strauss' definition of philosophy.

When we read such phrases as "l'immédiateté du vécu," we are inevitably reminded of the philosopher who dominated the French scene during the formative years of Lévi-Strauss: Henri Bergson. If we keep Bergson in mind as we read our "Finale" we cannot fail to discover many more Bergsonian expressions and they are far from limited to those things Lévi-Strauss detests and assimilates to philosophy and ritual. His references to the structural principle he espouses are also couched in phrases borrowed from that philosopher, such as "discontinuité," "découpage," "schématisme de la pensée," etc. Lévi-Strauss is convinced there is not an ounce of philosophy in him, especially Bergsonian philosophy. We can readily understand the cause of that belief. He and Bergson are literally poles apart. The two poles, however, are those of Bergson's metaphysics. If you turn these poles around, you understand better why the undifferentiated and differentiation mean so much to Lévi-Strauss, why he hates to find them in conjunction. Everything Bergson embraces Lévi-Strauss rejects; everything Bergson rejects Lévi-Strauss embraces.

One single sentence in our text says more than a long exegesis: "La fluidité du vécu tend constamment à s'échapper à travers les mailles du filet que la pensée mythique a lancé sur lui pour n'en retenir que les aspects les plus contrastés" (p. 603). If we had to guess the author, we would certainly name Bergson. It does more than sound like Bergson, it gives us his whole metaphysics in a nutshell. Bergson hoped that a more advanced science, led by biology, would understand the inadequacy of rigid differentiations and move to his side. Recent discoveries, especially that of the genetic code, have convinced Lévi-Strauss that the opposite must happen. Thanks to the genetic code, Lévi-Strauss can now put a name, he says, on that principle of discontinuity which governs the works of nature as well as of culture; this principle moves the entire universe and finally becomes conscious of itself, first in a crude mythological form, later in the works of science.

This association between genetics and mythology has an unexpected result; it permits a reappropriation by Lévi-Strauss of none other than the good old *élan vital* which needs only a slight adaptation before it can reappear as an *élan différenciateur*, perhaps, or *codificateur*:

En suivant des voies auxquelles on reproche d'être trop exclusivement intellectuelles, la pensée structuraliste recouvre ... et ramène à la surface de la conscience des vérités profondes et organiques. Seuls ceux qui la pratiquent connaissent, par expérience intime, cette impression de plénitude qu'apporte son exercice, et par quoi l'esprit ressent qu'il communie vraiment avec le corps. (p. 619)

The specific and generic consequences of the genetic code do not resemble the mythical representations of the undifferentiated and differentiation. This is equally true of language, of course, which operates through a smaller number of already discrete elements, not through the physical partitioning of some more or less homogeneous underlying substance. This is an objection that Lévi-Strauss himself brings up (p. 605). Myth represents only in a very imperfect fashion the process of intelligence and life. Between myth and the universal life-force, there is nevertheless a communication, a reciprocal affinity that is all the more remarkable for lacking the proper means of expression. Thus, Lévi-Strauss explicitly admits that even in myth there are representations of the undifferentiated which do not correspond to the "real" metaphysical drama he thinks modern science has uncovered, but this inadequacy becomes one more cause for admiration, whereas in the case of ritual the very same thing becomes an irritating artifice, a deplorable phoniness.

The similarities between Bergson and Lévi-Strauss are more than an amusing paradox; they reach down to the core of structuralism. The fact that Bergson privileges one pole of the metaphysical dualism and Lévi-Strauss the other makes little difference. The important thing is that, in each case, both reality and the mind have been replaced by a metaphysical principle. These two principles appear closely interrelated but are really independent. Reality being assimilated to a pure undifferentiation does not suggest in what manner it should be carved. It provides no guidelines to the differentiating principle which operates in the void. Any mode of differentiation is as good or as bad as any other.

When Lévi-Strauss becomes aware of the metaphysical substitutions we have just detected, he attributes them to mythology itself, he views them as a brilliant intuition of mythical thought and the end result is the same. If we examine still another facet of the structural practice, we will realize that the reading of mythology depends even more on metaphysics than our previous remarks have already made clear.

Take the myth which is dominated until the end by a character defined as the jaguar-woman. If this monster belonged in a ritual, she would probably appear as a mask, worn by one or several participants and we could dismiss her as the artificial piecing together of two creatures already differentiated by the language of myth, the jaguar and the woman. If she appeared only at the beginning of a myth, we could see her as a representation of the undifferentiated once more, but a legitimate one this time, a stepping-stone to the differentiation which is to follow and reconfirm the mutual separateness of jaguars and women. None of these two solutions is available, since the jaguar-woman has decided to stick around until the bitter end of the myth. This monster, it would appear, is not playing by the rules. She is no less perverse than ritual. She should be kicked out of the structuralist class-room. What is Lévi-Strauss going to do?

Lévi-Strauss remains imperturbable. He keeps on playing his binary game as if the jaguar-woman were an object like any other object. Why should it matter if the pawns are jaguars, if they are women, or if they are jaguar-women? Lévi-Strauss does not have to take such trifles into account. His structural principle has nothing to do with a real perception that discovers real objects in the real world. It is a pure differentiating principle that operates on a pure undifferentiated. He does not have to apologize, therefore, because the machine turns out jaguar-women from time to time rather than women that are only women and jaguars that are only jaguars. Who has ever said the products of differentiation should be the same for everybody? Who knows if we are not the victim of an ethnocentric fallacy when we demand a special treatment for the jaguar-woman? Can't we object, as we did in the case of ritual, that the jaguar and the woman are already distinguished by lan-guage? Possibly, but it is also possible that the original language of the myth treats the jaguar-woman as a genuinely independent entity. The combination of a horse and a human being is some-thing like the jaguar-woman but we call it a centaur, don't we? We do not say a horseman or, when we do, we mean something quite different.

The layman is lost in admiration. There must be something vastly scientific, he assumes, about a method that can disregard so superbly the questions that keep nagging our little minds. Why is *le fantastique* on the same footing with the real? The question cannot be asked any more because the real has disappeared. For all practical purposes the real is assimilated to the undifferentiated and human thought is explicitly assimilated to the principle of pure differentiation.

Le fantastique has been dissolved all right but in the most unscientific fashion. If the preceding observations are correct, *le fantastique* is divided into three fragments, and structuralism dis-poses of these fragments separately. Only in the case of ritual is *le fantastique* at least indirectly acknowledged as a disturbing ques-tion and unceremoniously discarded as contrary to the principles of human thought. The old anthropologists would have said that it was "irrational." Two fragments are left and they both belong to myth. They are both incorporated into the process of differentia-tion. The second one is swallowed up by the machine and it comes out looking like everything else; the first one provides the indispensable background for differentiation as a self-displaying process. In this dissolution of all fantastic elements, the dissolving agent is always the same; it is the metaphysical dualism borrowed from Bergson.

We have philosophical and ideological motivations for the one-sided treatment of both ritual and myth. These motivations are paramount but they operate within a context shaped by the history of anthropology. A brief glance at this history may be in order. At the beginning of the twentieth century, Lucien Lévy-Bruhl was led to postulate the existence of a "primitive mentality," unable to distinguish entities and categories which mature human thought can and must distinguish. Durkheim reacted against this view. The association between the kangaroo and a group of human beings does not signify a confusion between the two; rather it signifies a distinction between this first group and a second one which is associated, perhaps, with the wallaby. Symbolic thought demands both conjunction and disjunction. If the observer is not familiar with the conjunction, he is likely to concentrate unduly upon it; failing to perceive its disjunctive role, he will mistake it for a complete assimilation. Americans use animals for their political symbols; they do not confuse one another with real elephants and real donkeys.

Following the lead of Durkheim, Lévi-Strauss shows that much that formerly appeared senseless in primitive cultures really makes sense. And the sense is made through binary networks of symbolic conjunctions and disjunctions that can be methodically mapped out. If there is a "manifest destiny" of structuralism, it is to extend as far as possible the area of meaningfulness in the structural sense. In *Le Totémisme aujourd'hui*, Lévi-Strauss reaches the conclusion that the whole problem of totemic institutions is not only wrongly labelled but unreal.[3] The illusion that the so-called totemic cultures do not think like us and need to be set apart rests entirely on ethnocentric fallacies of the type I have outlined.

Lévi-Strauss speaks of his surprise when he found that Bergson had anticipated his own elegant dissolution of the totemic problem. Such a coincidence, Lévi-Strauss speculates, must come

---

[3] Claude Lévi-Strauss, *Le Totémisme aujourd'hui* (Paris: Presses universitaires de France, 1962).

from the very primitiveness of the philosopher's thinking, from an emotional empathy which puts this creature of instinct directly in touch with *la pensée sauvage*. The same intuition can only reappear at the other end of the intellectual tunnel, fully articulate this time, in the cold scientific glare of structuralism.[4]

We might have anticipated this miraculous agreement. Focusing as he does upon "la continuité du vécu," Bergson shows little interest in the various ways in which this continuity can be broken. If you bring to his attention something like totemic institutions, he will immediately realize that they are as far from his cherished immediacy as Socratic dialectics or medieval scholasticism. All modes of articulate thought allow this immediacy to slip from their grasp. Bergson will be inclined, therefore, to lump totemism with all the other modes as, of course, Lévi-Strauss also does.

Let us see, now, what happens with an investigator who is not Bergsonian in any form, not even in reverse. As a critic of the ethnocentric fallacy and an initiator of structuralism, Durkheim is especially appropriate. In some respects, his view of totemic names as "emblems" is even more destructive of the problem than that of Lévi-Strauss. At no point, however, does he substitute a metaphysical undifferentiated for the perception of the real world. As a consequence he finds himself asking concrete questions about the so-called undifferentiated. What can it be? What may have caused it?

Human experience is never such as to suggest the combinations and mixtures we find in totemic institutions. From the perspective of sense observation everything is diverse and discontinuous. Nowhere in nature do we see creatures mix their natures and metamorphose into each other. An *exceptionally powerful cause must have been present, therefore, to transfigure the real and make it appear under aspects which do not belong to it.*[5] (translation and italics mine)

Because he does not confuse the undifferentiated and differentiation with the two poles of a Bergsonian metaphysics, Durkheim *must* ask himself why primitive thought can have at the same time so many monsters and so many distinctions that are real.

---

[4] *Ibid.*, pp. 132-49.

[5] Emile Durkheim, *Les Formes élémentaires de la vie religieuse* (Paris: Presses universitaires de France, 1968), pp. 337-38.

Durkheim does not say that the Australian aborigines cannot distinguish a man from a kangaroo but he does not say either, that the proliferation of kangaroo-ancestors and jaguar-women poses no problem whatever. His position avoids both the extreme of the so-called primitive mentality, and the other extreme represented by structuralism and its various offspring. Durkheim's position may look at first like a timid compromise between two valorous knights-errant of anthropology who fearlessly radicalize the problematic. In reality, Durkheim's perspective is the only one from which the problem of culture, or the problem of language or, if you prefer, the problem of symbolic thought, becomes concrete.

Durkheim speaks of an *extremely powerful cause* which must make reality accessible to man and at the same time partly transfigures it; he suggests the same origin for primitive religion and for symbolic thought itself, a volcanic origin that makes reality appear both under aspects that belong to it and under aspects that do not belong to it. This view of the problem may well be the most precious legacy of Durkheim which later developments have obscured and pushed aside.

Lévi-Strauss perceives that the origin of symbolic thought is a legitimate theoretical question. He denies, however, that this question can be concretely investigated. As a proof of this, he mentions the failure of those who tried, the Freud of *Totem and Taboo* and Durkheim himself, who were unable, in the hypotheses they formulated, to divest themselves of the cultural rules and symbolicity for which they were trying to account. These failures are real but they do not mean the undertaking is meaningless. There is a lot to learn, anyway, both from Durkheim's idea of a collective *effervescence* and from Freud's idea of a primordial murder even if neither idea is an acceptable solution of the problem.

In my view, the achievements of Lévi-Strauss himself make a new attempt at solving the same problem more meaningful. His specific contribution, I believe, lies in these two categories of differentiation and undifferentiation which he has developed but which he cannot fully utilize because he turns them into metaphysical absolutes. When he insists on equating differentiation in myths with the process of "human thinking," he does not do justice to the conjunctive elements in his own symbolic network; we must not follow him when he says that myth alone is "good to think," when he excommunicates ritual from anthropology, and when he equates the undifferentiated with ritual.

Can the undifferentiated be equated with the fantastic elements in primitive religion? Not quite, but the two questions are closely related to each other. We have already suggested that mythical monsters, those conglomerates of differences, must be in some respects the verbal equivalent of the bizarre actions demanded by rituals such as incest, sex inversions, and reversal of social hierarchies, which have the undifferentiation of the community as their common denominator. We can consider all these phenomena as accidents of differentiation that suggest a real social crisis. If the undifferentiated cannot be a perverse "nostalgia for the immediate" or a legitimate allusion to some genuinely presymbolical no man's land, it can only allude to some kind of disorder, to a crisis of differences.

The structuralists would say that such speculations are idle talk because the nature of primitive societies and the absence of documents precludes any historical investigations. The possibilities I have in mind have nothing to do with a historical investigation. The only investigation that makes sense is still a structural one. There are many features in ritual behavior and in the fantastic elements of both myth and ritual that suggest the same type of crisis everywhere, a pattern of disintegration that transcends the historical uniqueness of specific incidents.

If we want to understand the nature of the ritual crisis, we must pay heed, I believe, to those aspects of rituals and prohibitions that suggest fierce mimetic rivalries and a reciprocal alienation that is constantly reinforced by a feedback effect until separate perceptions become jumbled together. If we observe the constant fascination with mirror effects and enemy twins, in primitive ritual as well as in primitive mythology, we will have to conclude that the undifferentiated has something to do with the symmetry of conflict, with a circular pattern of destructuration that must constitute a real threat. This would explain why primitive societies are almost as loath to think these matters through as structuralism itself. Their purpose is the same as Lévi-Strauss'—to redifferentiate the identical twins, to stop the crisis and replace the fearful symmetry of mimetic rivalry with the reassuringly static and manageable binary patterns to which structuralism limits its understanding of the religious text.

The possibilities I am trying to explore are often suggested by the myths and rituals which rarely speak of themselves as if they constituted an absolute beginning. Lévi-Strauss takes note of these suggestions but he rejects them as ridiculous. How could disorder generate order? he explicitly asks (p. 607). Not directly, of course, but why should the generative process be direct? Lévi-Strauss himself has often acknowledged, notably in *Anthropologie structurale I*, the key role played by some very ambiguous figures such as the North American *trickster* upon whom all the contradictions inherent not only in disorder but in the improbable conjunction of disorder and order appear to converge and to settle. These figures are highly exalted as mythical heroes, founding ancestors, even savior gods, but they may also be debased as cheats, transgressors and criminals. At the least, there will be something anomalous in them which bespeaks great misfortune as well as a high destiny.

If we assume that the mimetic crisis can be resolved through a still mimetic but unanimous transfer against an arbitrary victim, we can also be sure that the arbitrariness of the deed will escape the reconciled community. The victim should therefore acquire in retrospect all the features which are ascribed to the ambiguous mediators of mythology. In the eyes of the community, that victim will appear responsible both for the violence that raged when it was alive and for the peace that is restored by its death. It becomes the signifier of all relations between the members of the community, especially the worst and the best. We can understand, then, why all religious prescriptions can be referred to that ambiguous mediator—the prohibitions because their purpose is to avoid a recurrence of the crisis which the victim embodies, the rituals because they are a reenactment of the crisis not for its own sake but for the sake of the sacrificial resolution and the greater communal unity it is supposed to achieve. We can understand why a notion such as the sacred with its omnipotence both for the best and for the worst can develop from such episodes of "victimage."[6] If we only assume that the original transfer is effective, the interpretation of both conflictual and harmonious relations, inside and outside the community, must focus on the victim; all features of religious systems and religious behavior become intelligible.

The religious transfer is the fundamental fact which each religious community must interpret in its own way within the structural constraints that stem from the type of collective delusion it cannot fail to be. Far from being rigidly reductive, the

---

6 See my *La Violence et le sacré* (Paris: Grasset, 1972). An English translation will be published in 1977 by the Johns Hopkins Press.

hypothesis accommodates all the variants of religious systems, as well as their invariants. The element of victimage often remains half-visible, but it normally assumes only a secondary role, as if the game were dominated by the victim rather than the victimizers. The structuring poser of victimage remains hidden.

An examination of myths reveals that, at the moment of resolution, whenever it remains perceptible, a diversity of oppositions tends to give way to an *all against one* pattern which is treated, of course, by the structural analyst as one more binary differentiation of the usual type. This pattern recurs so frequently that the observer should suspect it may have a structural relevance. Even if the structuralists did isolate this pattern, their formalistic and metaphysical assumptions would prevent them from grasping its real power both as a peace maker and as a symbol maker.

If we look at the two myths mentioned in the preceding pages, we will see that both can be interpreted as the mythical surfacing of structurally misunderstood scapegoat phenomena. In the first myth, the overcrowding and confusion that prevails at the beginning is resolved by the elimination of a single element. Lévi-Strauss offers a purely logical interpretation of this process. This is what he does, too, in *Le Totémisme aujourd'hui*, with two other well-known myths. The genesis of "totemic" classifications is accounted for by the elimination of something in excess; *more space* is thus provided. In the case of each of these two myths, however, he acknowledges the presence of a greedy and indiscreet divinity, analogous to the Scandinavian Loki, whose ill-advised and pernicious action triggers the process of elimination. The god himself, in each case, is either the sum total or part of what is forcefully expelled.[7] Obviously an interpretation that would not be purely logical and spatial is possible; if this interpretation runs along the lines I propose it will make fully intelligible all the elements which structuralism is forced to leave out of account. The same is true, of course, of the jaguar-woman, that resilient monster who is finally brought to a sad end. After much mischief, she is thrown into a fire and burned to death by all the other characters united against her. This is the end of the myth and we must presume that order is (re)established.[8]

Collective victimage is a *hypothesis* regarding the origin of

---

[7] Lévi-Strauss, *Le Totémisme aujourd'hui*, pp. 25-37.
[8] Lévi-Strauss, *Du Miel aux cendres*, p. 313.

both primitive religion and symbolicity. The unanimous transfer and victimage to which all directly and indirectly observable religious systems can be traced must be the distant descendants of more elementary and unimaginable phenomena from which symbolic thought itself originates. The word *hypothesis* must not be interpreted as a precaution or a hesitation in the face of the current climate of opinion. According to one reviewer my theory so scandalously contradicts the current dogma that even I cannot fully believe in it and this is the reason I use the word *hypothesis*. The structuring power of victimage is necessarily *hypothetical* because no continuous line of empirical evidence, no linguistico-structural analysis will ever lead directly to it. This does not disqualify it at all since all religious themes are brought back to a single structural delusion which necessarily transfigures or eliminates its own generative mechanism.

The only relevant questions concern (1) the state of our knowledge at the present time; does it leave room for a hypothesis of the type I propose? (2) the power of the hypothesis to account for the anthropological data. The answer to the first question cannot fail to be yes since the results of both the empirical and the linguistico-structural approach are incomplete, unsatisfactory and irreconcilable. Some people will say that this impasse cannot be resolved until the time when all cultural problematic is dissolved into some kind of superchemistry.

The possibility of a successful hypothesis is more likely; it is this possibility which has come to pass each time a new discipline has managed to achieve a truly scientific status. If a significant breakthrough must occur, it will occur in the form of a hypothesis remote enough from the data to permit a real confrontation with them. The present hypothesis calls for such a confrontation. We must realize, however, that no hypothesis, however pertinent, will ever obtain a seal of approval from the dogmatic methodologies in which a prescientific discipline must trust. Dogmatic methodologies never have any use for fully explicit hypotheses.

This journal is not the place to demonstrate the anthropological value of my hypothesis. I must limit myself to the text at hand which is the "Finale" of *Mythologiques*. If my hypothesis is correct, if the origin and structure of symbolic forms are such as I claim, this text too should fall somehow under its jurisdiction, however remotely and mediately.

First, let us consider the problem of our text from a purely rational and scholarly perspective. I said that the "manifest destiny" of structuralism was to extend further and further the frontiers of meaning in the structural sense. The gist of my remarks is that the reach of structuralism has exceeded its grasp. Many disciples, direct and indirect, would deny this, of course, but Lévi-Strauss himself knows better. Our "Finale" is a long postponed encounter with those phenomena that do not respond properly to the structuralist method.

If a methodology is not universal, it must at least state unambiguously to which objects it does apply and to which it does not. If there are rebellious phenomena, it is imperative to show that they are not spread throughout the anthropological corpus; they must belong to some well-defined area easily separated from the rest. Lévi-Strauss must also show that these phenomena do not amount to some impenetrable mystery, or worse still, to some enigma that could be solved by means other than his method. Ideally, therefore, he must find a unique center of willful and sterile resistance to his structural reason.

In the "Finale" of *L'Homme nu*, Lévi-Strauss announces that he has found precisely what he needed, in ritual; this institution is a senseless revolt against the very essence of human intelligence and those who insist on taking ritual seriously can only share in the same delusion. This conclusion is untenable. It cannot be defended unless the data are seriously distorted. In order to validate the claims of his structuralist method, Lévi-Strauss needs this conclusion badly. If we look at these distortions, however, they do not suggest anything like a conscious manipulation or even careless expediency. They have a coherence of their own; they form a pattern systematic enough to be both less visible before we detect it and more visible afterwards than a calculated falsification or an accidental error could be.

Let us summarize that pattern once more. Lévi-Strauss takes all differentiation away from ritual and gives it to myth. He does the same thing with the undifferentiated but in reverse. What is taken away from ritual, myth must receive; what is taken away from myth, ritual must receive. The redistribution is symmetrical with one small but essential exception. In order to turn myth into the sacred temple of differentiation, some of the undifferentiated must be kept there, acknowledged as such, or almost as such.

How can we account for this remarkable pattern, and especially for that crucial ambiguity at the center of it, for the dual nature of the undifferentiated which is evil in bulk, so to speak, but becomes good and indispensable in smaller amounts at the beginning of myth? If we view the excommunication of ritual as the intellectual equivalent of the ritual expulsion, if we reread our text in the light of the anthropological hypothesis I have outlined, we will find that the systematic distortion of the anthropological data becomes intelligible. This application of the hypothesis will appear more appropriate if we think of the arbitrariness which characterizes the treatment of ritual and which duplicates exactly the arbitrariness of the victim in the hypothesis. Ritual, philosophy and even what Lévi-Strauss calls "structuralisme-fiction" are not really what Lévi-Strauss says they are, nor can they all be found together—or even separately—in the place where Lévi-Strauss seeks them out.

Ritual is expelled as the sole and complete embodiment of the undifferentiated. This expulsion is supposed to rid us once and for all of this "evil mixture" as Shakespeare would call it. And yet, a small quantity is needed to insure the transfiguration of myth. It is no longer the "evil mixture" but a most crucial component in the presentation of myth as an exemplary manifestation of human thinking. How can this transfiguration take place? If we confer the generative role upon the expulsion of ritual, we will see that the circulation and metamorphosis of the undifferentiated works exactly like the *sacra* of primitive religion. The victim appears to embody the violence of the crisis, interpreted as a bad and disruptive *sacrum* but metamorphosed by the expulsion into something still dangerous but beneficial and constructive, provided it is used in the right place, at the right time and in precisely measured quantities. Only priests or initiates can practice this delicate operation.

The undifferentiated is viewed as an infection that would contaminate the whole anthropological body if the affected limb were not speedily amputated. Since the undifferentiated is supposed to be entirely contained in ritual, it is entirely expelled by the expulsion of ritual. What we have at the beginning of myth is not some of the old stuff left over, even though, at the same time, it is still exactly the same thing—but the result of an alchemy that coincides with the "kathartic" effect of the expulsion. The deadly fermentation that threatened the whole body is gone; in its place we have a pinch of yeast that causes the whole textual dough to rise. Left to itself, the undifferentiated is pure disintegration; once transmuted by the expulsion, it holds the key to the structure of myth as a self-organizing system. In this expulsion of the various *bêtes noires*, a negative force is partly spent and partly channelled into the directions required for the reorganization of the text on a basis acceptable to structuralism.

The undifferentiated of Lévi-Strauss works exactly like the *pharmakon* in Plato's *Phaedrus* as explicated by Derrida.[9] It is the drug which is both bad and good at the same time: in large amounts it acts like poison; in the right doses prescribed by the right doctor, it becomes the medicine that restores our health. The reference to Plato is especially appropriate. The most striking parallel to our expulsion of ritual comes in *The Republic* with the treatment of the poet who is adorned as a sacrificial victim before being ordered to leave. To Plato, most poetry—and mythology—is a mimetic loss of differentiation and the concomitant production of undifferentiated monsters. All art is closely related to the undifferentiation of orgiastic rituals. The fact that philosophy and mythology are on opposite sides of those particular fences is unimportant; the scapegoats cannot fail to be arbitrary. The purpose of the expulsion remains constant. Plato, like Lévi-Strauss, wants to make his perfect city safe for differentiation. Knowledge and differentiation are the same thing. We must not be surprised if the inverted Bergsonism of Lévi-Strauss sounds like a Platonism right side up.

Ritual, contrary to what Lévi-Strauss believes, is an earlier effort to expel the "evil mixture" and make culture safe for differentiation. Paradoxically, therefore, the Lévi-Straussian expulsion of the undifferentiated, just like the Platonic expulsion of mimesis, pursues the same objective as ritual. This observation can be generalized. The horrified recoil from primitive ritual and religion stems from the same impulse as religion itself, in the new circumstances brought about by this very religion. We must abandon the linear logic that sees the anti-religious text as independent from the religious text it pretends to "demystify." In reality the religious text is a first violent recoil from crude forms of violence; it is also a complex economy in which this same violence is in part assuaged by sacrifice, in part camouflaged, ignored and transfigured.

Contrary to what Lévi-Strauss believes, ritual is a first effort

---

[9] Jacques Derrida, "La Pharmacie de Platon," in *La Dissémination* (Paris: Seuil, 1972), pp. 71-197.

to expel the "evil mixture." Thus, the Lévi-Straussian text is generated by a new expulsion, in many respects identical to the ritual one; what is expelled is the expulsion itself, but so it is already in the religious forms. The truth of the expulsion is the essential taboo of ,human culture; far from transgressing it, the second-generation expulsion reinforces this taboo. This explains why this metaphysical operation produces effects structurally similar to the religious expulsion; these effects generate a new text, a duplicate of the religious form in which the metaphysical notions, and more specifically the undifferentiated, display the same paradoxical qualities and function exactly like the former *sacra*.

All postritual institutions are generated, it appears, by these second-generation expulsions which expel the former agent of expulsion. This is true of the theater, of philosophy and also of the judicial system, political institutions, etc. In all these forms, the process of "expelling the expulsion," of effacing the traces, is a continuous one which takes these forms farther and farther away from their origin. They are more and more estranged from their real subject and yet they can never really take leave of that subject.

The greatness of modern anthropology is that indirectly, no doubt, unknowingly and still unsuccessfully but nevertheless significantly, it reaches back toward those cultural forms that can throw the most decisive light upon the generative process of all cultural texts. The discipline of anthropology was fascinated at first by primitive religion. In recent years, however, that fascination has subsided. The history of that discipline seems to repeat the history of all postritual institutions or texts. With structuralism, that evolution has accelerated and it is, so to speak, legitimized. The great religious questions are out. By purging anthropology of its "evil mixture," Lévi-Strauss tries to rid it of those elements which still remain intractable after a century of speculation. It is true that these speculations, so far, have not produced the expected results. But it is better to acknowledge the failure than to declare the problem meaningless.

The problem was certainly badly formulated, and the Lévi-Straussian purge, perhaps, can contribute to a better formulation. The greatness of Lévi-Strauss is that his text still bears the marks of this arbitrary purge. At least indirectly, therefore, this text still communicates with everything it disallows. This will not be true, I am afraid, of the anthropological "discourse" Lévi-Strauss has made possible. This discourse can go on endlessly without being interrupted by any disturbing questions. From now on, we will learn everything there is to learn about the contrasted significance of "rare," "medium-rare" and "well-done" in the cannibalistic feast, but of cannibalism itself there will be no question. Like our prejudice against the jaguar-woman, our refusal to eat human flesh will be treated as an ethnocentric fallacy we must learn to overlook.

This process of anthropological neutralization resembles closely what has happened to a great deal of literary criticism in the last thirty years, both in this country with the great war against "the intentional fallacy" and in the French-speaking countries with the so-called "thematic," then with the "structuralist," criticism. As Leo Bersani observes of Georges Poulet:

The image of a circle may be recurrent in literature, but no interesting literary work can be adequately discussed in terms of its metaphors of "centers" and "circumferences." And even the categories of time and space in, for example, Proust can themselves be made intelligible only if they are placed in relation to other things in the work (jealousy and snobbery, which Poulet doesn't even mention), that is, considered as metaphorical terms of a larger system in which affectivity is infinitely more than geometric. [10]

It is supremely significant, of course, that the themes eliminated from the reading of Proust be jealousy and snobbery. These themes are the equivalent of ritual in the anthropological text; erotic and social discrimination are the specifically Proustian modes of expulsion. Once more it is a former agent of expulsion which is expelled and this expulsion generates a critical discourse free from all traces of "evil mixture," totally sheltered from potentially disruptive questioning.

One can show, I believe, that the parallelism between the transmutation of literary criticism and that of anthropology stems from a second-generation expulsion which drowns all decisive questions in some form of metaphysical idealism. What is unique with Lévi-Strauss is the scrupulous exactness of his Bergsonism in reverse. The dualism itself, in forms that may vary with the individual borrower, is the common denominator for all those

---

[10] "From Bachelard to Barthes," in *Issues in Contemporary Literary Criticism*, ed. Gregory T. Polletta (Boston: Little, Brown and Co., 1973), p. 97.

combinations of philosophy, ideology, literary criticism and social science which, under diverse labels, have dominated the French scene for many a year.

Sartre undoubtedly played a pivotal role in this affair. His well-known misreading of Heidegger, that famous *contresens* to which we owe *Being and Nothingness*, truly amounts to a first and historically decisive relapse into Bergsonian metaphysics, disguised by the Germanic terminology. It does not really matter if the earlier "flux" freezes into a motionless *en-soi*. It does not matter if the agent of differentiation becomes the negativity of a *pour-soi*. The important point is that the relationship between the two poles remains indeterminate, behind an appearance of determination. Sartre is the only one who ever explicitly recognized this indeterminacy. He calls it *freedom*. He almost gave the whole game away even before it started. He has been rebuked for this ever since.

As long as this indeterminacy is clearly understood, only avowedly subjective idealists will be attracted to the metaphysical dualism. And it is, indeed, in a mood of avowedly subjective idealism that *Les Temps modernes* was launched. The indeterminacy, however, is likely to remain unperceived. The relationship between the two poles is always expressed in pairs of terms that do not make sense if they are employed separately, such as the *pour-soi* and the *en-soi*, the *découpage* and the *non-découpé*, differentiation and the undifferentiated. These pairs of words make us feel that the relationship must be very close, even inextricable. It looks like a serious matter, something that cannot be taken lightly. In reality this relationship is one of undefined and undefinable distortion on both sides, even of complete betrayal. Even if we wanted to, we could not take it into account. Structures can be studied as if they were completely autonomous, which is the only manner, of course, in which we can study structures and even conceive of such things as structures.

Social scientists are always on the lookout for a position that will reconcile their awareness of cultural relativism with their belief in the unity of knowledge, a belief they cannot discard without discarding the scientific enterprise itself. As long as its real nature is not clearly understood, the metaphysical dualism inherited from Bergson and Sartre appears to square that particular circle. Singularities do not have to be silenced and yet oppositions do not have to be resolved. It does not matter if the stuff on the outside is solid, liquid or in-between. It does not matter if it is lumpy, grainy or smoothly homogenized. What really matters is that it gives no indication whatever of how it should be carved; it provides no guidelines to the process of differentiation. With Sartre, for instance, as in the Lévi-Straussian mythology, the *en-soi* is perfectly meaningless until it is given meaning by the *pour-soi*. This meaning is already a structure which is called the *project*. We cannot even ask, in the last analysis, if some projects are better than others. Some people see their colleagues as colleagues when they get to the office in the morning, others see them as jaguar-women. Everybody is entitled to his own project and *honni soit qui mal y pense*.

The shift from the *existential* to the *phenomenological* and to the *structural* corresponds to a gradual move away from the first pole, a move led by Sartre himself, who soon gave up the nauseous embrace of the *en-soi* for analyses of the *pour-soi*'s projects. The structural label has less to do with a specific method, or methods, than with the fusion of the second pole with some social or anthropological discipline. This combination gives the second pole the added "weight" needed to tip the scales in its favor. Instantly, the borrowed discipline seems to achieve a high degree of autonomy and scientific maturity. Thus, Gestalt psychology, ethnology and structural linguistics, together with a constantly revamped Freudianism and Marxism, were successively or simultaneously brought into play.

All the loudly advertised "revolutions" of the past thirty years have never changed anything essential; they simply tend to eliminate the first pole entirely and to widen in the extreme the definition of the second. The evolution itself and its effects are both entirely predictable. It is obvious, for instance, that there cannot be any *subject* but the structure itself. As long as the arbitrary *découpage* that determines the structural field remains under the influence of classical philosophy, or literature, the individual will appear omnipotent because the structure will extend no farther than his reach. When the emphasis shifts to the social sciences and to language, the structure exceeds anything we can call individual and the impotence, even the inexistence of the individual subject, follows as inexorably as its total omnipotence in the previous phase.

We can also expect that, in due time, the whole mood of the enterprise is going to change. As the disciples contemplate the works of their masters, enthusiasm gives way to lassitude, even to a spirit of rebellion, to a desire for new expulsions. All these solipsistic structures lined up on the cultural shelves of *la modernité*, be they books, paintings, myths, entire cultures or anything else, begin to look and to taste like canned goods on the shelves of a supermarket. When all the sublimely "unique" "worlds" of count- less individual writers are neatly stashed away in the pages of critical anthologies, each occupying roughly the same amount of space, the undivided worship briefly granted to each in turn cannot fail to evoke the treatment reserved to tourist-class passengers on a fully loaded commercial airplane. We have better reasons than we think to be vociferous in our dislike of the *société de consomma- tion*. We are an integral part of it. We cannot respect all differences equally without in the end respecting none.

To a Lévi-Strauss, the infinitely diverse products of the sym- bolic function testify to the unlimited power of man to create order out of chaos. To others, this same diversity testifies to man's inability to reach even a stable illusion, a permanent fiction, let alone any ultimate truth. In this disenchanted and subversive mood, the temptation will be irresistible for the investigator still faithful to the method, to turn it into a weapon against the whole Western industry of knowledge and finally against itself. To the Michel Foucault of *Les Mots et les choses*, each period in the old "history of ideas" is a structure floating in the void, like the Lévi-Straussian structure, or the Sartrian project here called an *episteme*. When the analysis reaches down to the observer's own time and to his own structuralist *episteme*, the scholar's enterprise vacillates on its pedestal to the obvious delight, this time, of this particular scholar who seems primarily intent on a most scholarly burial of scholarship itself.

An illusion of long standing is now dissolving, the illusion that a reconciliation has been achieved between the autonomy of "struc- tures" and the requirement of a universally valid context in which to study these structures. The conditions of a genuine science have never been met. Foucault clearly perceives this fact but he does not seem to perceive that the failure is that of a metaphysical system only. To conclude as he does that no science of man is possible, that the very idea must be a passing phase, is an illegitimate extrapolation. And that extrapolation obviously results from a continued belief in the old metaphysics. Foucault correctly appraises the limitations of this system but he confuses them with the absolute limits of human language and of our power to know.

Lévi-Strauss deplores this nihilism: he attributes it to "structuralisme-fiction," a loose application of his method (p. 573). As a response, in our "Finale" of *L'Homme nu*, he hardens all his previous positions; his differentiating principle becomes more isolated and abstract than ever. He reinforces in his own work the very features which lead to the attitudes he deplores. The same epistemological nihilism moves the later work of Gilles Deleuze. His fluxification of all differences, in *L'Anti-Oedipe*, is a parodic mimicry and a confusion of the structural gesture par excellence: the differentiation of the flux. [11] Differentiation itself, this time, turns undifferentiated, and the two together, more sacred than ever, are supposed to herald the schizophrenic liberation of our structuralist and capitalistic society.

The all-purpose differentiating machine is beginning to look like a played-out toy, a primitive noisemaker, perhaps, that must be agitated more and more wildly to keep the public and even its own users at least mildly interested. The metaphysical dualism is disintegrating from the inside but it still holds sway. It is natural for the entire venture to end up in the current solipsistic idealism of the linguistic structure.

We are constantly told these days that each interpretation is a new text and that for every text, there is an unlimited number of interpretations, each no more and no less valid than the next. We are constantly told of the irremediable loss that occurs even in the most careful translation from one language to another. Everybody says so; no one ever says anything else. Everybody by now should be convinced and there must be some other reason than our need for enlightenment in these sempiternal objurgations. There can be only one reason. We live in a world more unified every day by science and technology. The weight of evidence against the current view of language is so formidable that it needs no spokesman to be heard. Our unanimous chorus is not really able to cover the unacknowledged voice.

It is interesting to note that Lévi-Strauss, in theory, wants no part in this chorus. Only the natural sciences flourish, he says, *because in them only, the symbols and the referents are really adequate to each other.* The sorry state of the social sciences comes from their inability to emulate that ideal (p. 574). This adequacy is not an exclusive monopoly of advanced science with its highly mathematized language. It must obtain in large areas of

---

[11] Gilles Deleuze, *L'Anti-Oedipe* (Paris: Editions de Minuit, 1972).

even the most primitive cultures; otherwise, techniques would not be successful and could not be transmitted from generation to generation. The people would simply perish. From the technique of irrigation in ancient Egypt to the recipe for *boeuf bourguignon*, there is an immense linguistic domain whose practitioners never experience that titillating *glissement du signifié sous le signifiant* which is quite real, no doubt, in some domains, but which cannot be presented as characteristic of all language.

Lévi-Strauss acknowledges this fact, too. Unfortunately, these healthy theoretical views have no effect on the practice of structural analysis. Even if it is legitimate at some stage in the analysis of a myth to place side by side all the entities it differentiates, jaguar-women and all, it cannot be methodologically sound to assimilate, once and for all, those objects which can have a real referent, and those which cannot. The sciences Lévi-Strauss admires did not reach their present state of eminence by disregarding the difference between real percepts and hallucinations.

When we turn language into a prison-house, to use an expression of Fredric Jameson, [12] we ignore its true mystery, just as much as when we take it for granted, when we assume it is always perfectly adequate to its task. The true mystery is that language is both the perfectly transparent milieu of empiricism and the prison-house of linguisticism. Sometimes it is the one, sometimes it is the other; often it is an inextricable mixture of both.

No wonder some philosophers tried, and failed, to separate the linguistic wheat from the linguistic chaff. Even after we get rid of jaguar-women and other monsters—and the achievement should not be underestimated since it makes the natural sciences possible—our power to distinguish real objects, to fashion symbols that are adequate to their referents, seems to weaken as we turn back upon ourselves, as we try to understand the distinctions we make in the social, in the cultural and in the religious fields. The hypothesis I propose makes these difficulties understandable. If the power of man to distinguish anything is rooted in the most arbitrary of all our distinctions, in the sacralization of collective victims, if residual forms of victimage and sacralization are still operative among us, it is inevitable that objectivity will be most difficult to achieve as we reach closer and closer to the source of

---

[12] Fredric Jameson, *The Prison-House of Language* (Princeton: Princeton Univ. Press, 1972).

all symbolicity. Logical and philosophical means alone will never solve the problem. This does not mean a solution cannot be achieved, but the only hope to achieve it lies in the discovery of the origin and true nature of symbolicity. The problem is one with the enigma of primitive religion and the solution lies in a theory of the spontaneous scapegoat victim as the original symbol.

From the standpoint of the various trends that dominate the intellectual scene at the present time, this hypothesis inevitably appears marginal, eccentric. There are signs that it may not remain so forever but these signs are still scattered in works of very different inspiration and their unity is difficult to perceive. Among the more recent signs, all those critical works should be included which suggest some relationship, however indirect and tenuous, between human conflict and the principle of form, or structure. I read some texts of Jacques Derrida as such a sign. Another one, in my view, is the *pharmakos* archetype in the criticism of Northrop Frye. [13]

A third and most remarkable figure in the present context is Kenneth Burke. He anticipated some of the most interesting intuitions of recent years on the nature of symbolicity, yet he never succumbed to the seduction of the metaphysical dualism that limits the scope of these intuitions, on the other side of the Atlantic Ocean. As a consequence, Burke effectively encounters problems that remain invisible in the context of the free-floating solipsistic structure.

Burke asserts that a "principle of victimage" is implicit in the nature of drama. He takes it for granted, legitimately I believe (but surprisingly, in view of the general tenor of Aristotelian criticism), that the notion of *katharsis* refers to a process of victimage. In *Coriolanus*, Shakespeare consciously provides his hero with all the ambiguous qualities which make a good scapegoat. [14] These qualities are those enumerated by Aristotle in his *Poetics* and they are really a transposition of the requirements for a good sacrificial victim. Since tragic heroes normally come from religious myth and ritual, one would like to see the Burkean reading of tragedy expanded into a theory of those religious institutions

---

[13] See my "Lévi-Strauss, Frye, Derrida and Shakespearean Criticism," *Diacritics*, 3, No. 3 (1973), 34-38.

[14] Kenneth Burke, *"Coriolanus—and the Delights of Faction,"* in *Language as Symbolic Action* (Berkeley: Univ. of California Press, 1966), pp. 81-97.

which are based on explicit forms of victimage, like the *pharmakos* ritual of the Greeks.

In the eyes of Burke, violence and victimage result from a desire for a form too perfect and therefore from an abuse of the formal principle; they are not essential to that principle itself. Victimage follows from the form, in other words, but the reverse is not true: the form does not follow from victimage. Even if the principle of victimage is present in Burke's definition of man, that "symbol-using and mis-using animal," it will be there only as a "codicil." [15] Its position remains marginal, eccentric. Massive evidence from the anthropological data demands, I believe, that it be moved to the center, that it be made the origin of symbolicity.

---

[15] *Ibid.*, p. 16.

Intentionality
and the Literary Object

Ralph Freedman

—For W. K. Wimsatt

I

Two relationships dominate critical thought: the relationship between the poet and his persona or mask, and the relationship between language derived from experience (i.e., empirical reference) and the poem itself. These questions merge in critical discourse, but both determine the attitudes of poets and critics alike. On the one hand, we confront the living person who, with Virginia Woolf, falls in and out of love and gets through the day from lunch to dinner. On the other hand, we encounter the aesthetic persona who has transformed his love and his day into an objective or generalizing image. The terms of judgment and the issues up for debate have changed considerably—in the larger historical perspective since Aristotle and in the narrower perspective of the past thirty years—yet the crucial question has remained: How does the poet relate to the poem he himself has created?

One of the basic problems of criticism, then, still focuses on the work within the poet and on the poet within the work. Can we actually think of the poet's mind as separate from his work or are they both part of the same consciousness? We may dissolve poet and poem into linguistic or psychological elements; we may search for the aesthetic experience by chasing clues through corridors of minds or fields of genres. But the primary question continues to engage us: how do the poet's intentions correspond to those distinct (and perhaps autonomous) intentions in the work? Clearly, intention as a crucial part of the literary meaning is reflected in the poem's language, but it may also make itself known through other nonverbal conventions—actions and images not reducible to verbal expressions or forms. At the same time, it vibrates within the poet himself, in his passion or belief rendered accessible through the poet's peculiar discourse. It is my desire to show that the poet's mind in relation to his art—and his art in relation to his mind—can be understood only by assuming that both relate to one another as intimately connected yet separate entities.

It is assumed, then, that the concept of intentionality entails the existence of an independent literary object. But this assumption bears further explanation. Clearly, no one would deny that the poet's psychological and social circumstances, and those of his world, are always somehow mirrored in his language. Why then project the need for an independent object? But the real question is not whether a relationship exists between the poet's mind and *any* set of words, but whether it exists between his mind and a peculiarly *poetic* set of words. Therefore, only by examining how the poet's language has been formed can we understand the particular relevance of his life and intentions to the text under review. This assumption is, of course, subject to challenge, for it implies that the work created by the poet has its own distinct mode of existence.[1] It suggests that the poet's language is quite different from the words the poet uses when ordering his dinner and different as well from the discourse of history and social science— that indeed it is unique as an aesthetic creation whose nature we must examine.

II

Our first example is served by an emblematic poem of the sixteenth century: *Dizain* XIV of Maurice Scève's *Délie*, in which a

---

[1] The term is used in René Wellek's sense. See René Wellek and Austin Warren, *Theory of Literature*, 3rd ed. (New York: Harcourt, Brace, and World, 1962), pp. 142 ff.

palpable moment of passion "shines through" a pictorial image.
The poem begins:

> Elle me tient par ces cheveulx lyé,
> Et ie [je] la tien par ceulx là mesmes prise.
> Amour subtil au noud s'est allié
> Pour *se* devaincre une si ferme prise:
>
> She holds me by this hair bound
> And I hold her by this same (hair) captive.
> Subtle Amor has allied himself to this knot
> To tie it into so firm a catch.[2]

This scene is an *emblem*—a formal picture. The experience,
even as it involves the figure of Amor, is intensely felt. Its sexual-
ity is discernible beneath the verbal pattern. Yet the feeling is
expressed through general conventions caught in the emblem and
hence neutralized. As the entire structure of *Délie* is controlled by
rigorous prosody and equally rigorous Platonic conventions, this
particular *dizain*, too, gives evidence of a deliberately controlled
form suggested by tight rhetoric and a symmetrical design. Indeed,
this hermetically enclosed regularity, superimposed upon a rich
tapestry of feeling, has earned Scève the reputation of being, in
Sainte-Beuve's words, so obscure as to be almost unreadable.[3] Yet
the reader discerns simultaneously the sexual dilemma and the
intellectually derived form.

The poem begins with an accent upon *her*—the Lady holding
the poet by means of the hair is an allusion to, yet reversal of,
traditional attitudes. The firmness of the grasp, and its odd mutual
quality, is exemplified by the double action: in holding him
bound, she is simultaneously held. This is a rhetorical figure, to be

---

[2] The ten lines of French text printed on these pages are from *Délie.
Object de plaus haulte vertu*, in *The 'Délie' of Maurice Scève*, ed. I. D.
McFarlane (Cambridge: At the University Press, 1966), p. 126. McFarlane's
use of sixteenth-century spelling has been retained, except that "u's" have
been replaced by "v's," and "v's" by "u's" for the sake of clarity. The
translations are mine. I am most grateful to my friends, Florence and Kurt
Weinberg for their gracious advice.

[3] *Tableau historique et critique de la poésie française et du théâtre
français au XVIe siècle*, ed. Jules Troubat, *Oeuvres* (Paris: Alphonse Lemerre,
1876), I, 75*n*. See also a more general remark, p. 91*n*.

sure, but it is also redolent with personal feeling that strains
against the emblematic form: the poet has caught her who holds
him captive by the very nature of his dubious conquest. For the
mutual entanglement is countered by the poet's adversary, Amor,
who ties the knot of love. His action, though ostensibly unin-
tended, had a devastating effect:

> Combien qu'ailleurs tendist son entreprise,
> Que de vouloir deux d'un feu tourmenter.

> No matter how much his act might tend elsewhere
> Than to wish to torment two in one fire.

Focusing on Amor's intervention, Scève moves to a fuller knowledge of his and Délie's predicament as he completes the rhetorical
gesture. The hair, which in an analogous poem Petrarch had
likened to the golden fire of the sun (and his Laura therefore to
the source of light), has become a fire in which both are tormented—the conventional fire of hell.[4] Whatever Amor's intentions
may have been, the mutual fire has been created as that pit in
which the lovers are caught, held by the hair that binds
them together. A specific vision emerges, both personal and conventionally determined: mutually holding each other, joined in
their attraction and antagonism, the lovers are tormented in the
single fire of their infernal passion. Moreover, Amor's machinations
take on the quality of a diabolical experiment as Scève broadens
the image to place the two lovers in a pit:

---

[4] See Francesco Petrarca:

> L'aura soave al sole spiega e vibra
> L'auro ch'Amor di sua man fila e tesse
> Lá da' belli occhi, e de le chiome stesse
> Lega 'l cor lasso, e i lievi spirti cribra.

> The mellow aura in the sun displays
> The gold that Love himself both spins and weaves
> From the fair eyes, and with the same hair preys
> On my sad heart and my frail spirit cleaves.

Sonnet CXCVIII, "In Laura's Lifetime," in Petrarch, *Sonnets and Songs*,
Italian-English ed., trans. Anna Maria Armi (New York: Grosset and Dunlap,
1968), pp. 290-91.

Car (& vray est) pour experimenter
Dedans la fosse à mys & Loup, & Chievre,
Sans se povoir l'un l'aultre contenter,
Sinon respondre a mutuelle fiebrve.

For (and it is true) to experiment
Into a pit (he) has placed Wolf and Goat
Without either being able to satisfy the other
Except by responding to their mutual fever.

On the surface, the argument is essentially literary: the knot tied by Amor becomes an allegorical pit and fire in which the lovers are joined. It also alludes to the Christian hell, turning the spiritual, golden sunlight which Petrarch viewed in his Lady's hair into an infernal flame in which both lovers are caught. But in this latter sense, the action is fed by an intense feeling which we can only infer. In a poem by the Petrarchan poet, Tebaldeo, from whom Scève drew part of his formal inspiration, wolf and goat were, more conventionally, wolf and lamb, anticipating the Second Coming. But when Scève substituted goat for lamb, he changed not just ruminants and levels of discourse. Rather, he revealed a world of personal feeling while continuing to focus on an emblem of traditional figures. *Chievre* ("goat"), representing lust, is endowed with its own capacity for aggression. Délie, then, is both victim and aggressor, a mirror image of the poet himself. No wonder that they are caught in a mutual fire which neither can appease. The entire sequence is a well-rounded argument within a perfectly symmetrical form. But there is no way of mistaking the feeling beneath these emblematic conventions. Scève evoked a craggy interior landscape from an outwardly monolithic form.

The appearance of traditional Amor places the poet's emotion within the context of the literary object. An allegorical figure is introduced into the suggestive scene of two lovers caught by the same hair. Subtle Amor, predatory wolf, rapacious goat—together they crystallize the personal experience. Hence we need not ask who Délie was in the life of that strange poet at the court of Marguerite de Navarre. It is more significant to know that her name was derived from Virgil's Diana-Delia, that she embodied the ideal of *vertu*, and that her name was an anagram for *L'Idée*. But who has ever shared the same hold on hair with a Platonic Idea and, in being held, has been held by her as well? However conventional these figures are in their Renaissance context, something blooded and alive is suggested. Though the indebtedness to Petrarch is clear—we have noted the very image of the hair and its relation to fire—it is difficult to visualize *that* poet and his Laura in the same pit and fire, holding one another by each other's hair and responding endlessly to the fever of their compulsions. Yet Scève rendered all this impersonal, not just through the action of the psyche but through external literary and rhetorical forms which are gathered up in the tradition of the emblem. Within the confines of a ritualistic, heraldic picture, *L'Idée* and self, wolf and goat, are rendered allegorically meaningful. They are neutralized and turned into literary objects while at the same time evoking a living mind.

Despite the vibrant self-knowledge that lives within Maurice Scève's rigid poem, it is also always a conventionally defined object from which the living sensibility must be inferred. But in more recent poetry, traditional forms (whether produced by convention or myth) perform a different function. The search for mythological equivalences in poets like Blake, Hölderlin, or Keats, appears as a post-Renaissance, post-neoclassical effort to retain a balanced relationship between poet and mask. The poet is becoming a significant instrument in the conversion of life into art as the poem's distance from poet and reader is shortened. We can only *infer* Scève's agony through Amor, Wolf, and Goat. But in most modern poetry a different stance is taken. The poet's world is revealed through his own persona and the relation between self and form has been subtly altered. It was in the eighteenth century, in its prerevolutionary ferment of ideas and in its continued struggle to preserve the firm outlines of the Age of Reason, that this issue was joined.

III

We turn from the detached *emblem* in a sixteenth-century poem to its more problematic theoretical exploration by an eighteenth-century critic—Denis Diderot. It is more problematic because the very notion of depicting and transforming images into art now implicates the self as a distinct entity. For Scève, the emblem mediated between feeling and poetry; for Diderot, who used the same term, it performed a significantly different function.

Two contrasting currents in the eighteenth century define our situation. One was empiricism with its stress on the primacy of sense experience as received by the individual self. The other continued a neoclassical world view defined in terms of the Age of Reason, a view based on a conception of the world as a rationally analyzable whole. Of the two, empiricism was messier but less imperious. There were no clear-cut categories, but the meaning of life was not compressed into formulae. Society, like nature, poetry, or art, was not an independent world but a world present to a living self whose very nearness to life was vouchsafed by its direct involvement. The poet's mind, then, was engaged in his world and art through his organs of sense which received and transmitted feelings and ideas. We all know the importance of this dual heritage to the fiction of Goethe or Sterne, or to Rousseau's *Confessions*. On the one hand, the sensibility or consciousness of the self moved into the foreground. On the other hand, the inevitable loss of an independent body of standards removed objectivity and generality. How to restore the world beyond the self without losing the immediacy of sense experience as a standard for art became the crucial problem at this moment in the development of modernity.

Most significant at this juncture, therefore, was a critical orientation which discerned both the advantages and the disadvantages of empirical philosophy and measured them against a more traditional point of view in which the art object remained distinct, independent of any consciousness. Critics from Voltaire to Dr. Johnson confronted a paradox: stress on consciousness, whether on the poet's genius or the reader's taste, led to a dissolution of poems into linguistic or mental configurations. Ultimately, it entailed the dissolution of the mind as well, for, as David Hume showed, the existence of a unified consciousness cannot be proved by empirical means. Paradoxically, then, immediate consciousness of the self ultimately involved the loss both of the self and its object (in this case the poem) as well as the worlds and other selves it embodied. The greatest loss, however, was that of a communality, of a general sharing of conventions and strictures basic to poetic experience.

In response to this paradox Diderot formulated his particular view of aesthetic language. He saw that both the poem as a linguistic entity, and the poet as a user of language, had their intentions. But this reasoning could also lead to doubt in the poem's independent existence. As a result, Diderot based his theory on the principles of John Locke and the Comte de Condillac, while trying to retain firm standards by which forms and genres of literature could be defined. He developed a theory of art from a linguistic analysis of the interaction between impulse and effect peculiar to poetic language. Like I. A. Richards, who sought a similar solution in our time, he exhibited what Geoffrey Hartman, in describing Richards, has called a "romantic classicism."[5] This term aptly describes Diderot's paradoxical fix. His empirical bent led him to the question of what language can do. In his "Letter on the Deaf and Dumb," he used the sign language of the deaf—a pictorial, hence immediately sensory (nonrational) form of communication—as a means of defining literary art as well. In fact, the picture emerges as a middle ground between the mind's fleeting impressions and the possibility of more permanent forms.

It is at this point that we again encounter our *emblem* in the new setting of psychological exploration. It is derived from the recognition that while mental life is multifarious, the mind always acts in a single instant. We see an object like a mountain or a piece of gold, judge it beautiful, and desire its possession in a single instant, yet its description would be drawn-out and complex. Distinguishing between a state of mind and a (linguistic) account of it—one instantaneous and spatial, the other consecutive—Diderot developed his notion of the emblem. It catches and reflects the poet's meaning; a painting of its *denotatum*, it pulls together multiple perceptions and composes forms immediately accessible at a single glance.[6] Scève's emblems had performed the same function, but for Diderot that function was made possible by the activity of a perceiving mind through whose consciousness the emblem was formed. At the same time, since they are created by poetic language, Diderot must account for the progression of the words by which these syllables are formed. He therefore introduced a further term, the *hieroglyph*, which is less easily defined. Hieroglyphs are syllabic units—also conceived visually as reflections of natural objects (and their perception by the mind). Moments of perceived form, they are distributed among long and short syllables and thus create motion within the emblematic picture. But since the syllable is also the basic unit of French prosody, the function of these hieroglyphs is also tonal and musical. They create the link

---

[5] "I. A. Richards and the Dream of Communication," in *The Fate of Reading and Other Essays* (Chicago: Chicago Univ. Press, 1975), p. 22.

[6] Denis Diderot, *Oeuvres complètes* (Paris: Garnier frères, 1875), I, 369 ff.

between the visual image (appropriate to an essay on deaf-mutes) and the projection of sound within the movement of poetry. Indeed, it is one of the brilliant paradoxes of this essay that the sequence of hieroglyphs, rendering the perceived forms as visual images, also suggests the music and prosody of poetry. But it also provides a workable concept that regards the function of poetry in an empirical way. Translations from one language to another illustrate Diderot's point vividly: in a good translation the total emblem is not contradicted by the syllabic "imitations" of nature perceived by the poet's mind; in a poor translation it is.[7]

As both image and sound, the relationship between Diderot's emblems and his hieroglyphs reflected the tension within poetry as both image and voiced sound. Unlike Lessing, who separated space and sound, Diderot kept them together within the same linguistic units and indeed allowed the same concept (the hieroglyph) to reflect both dimensions at once. This is especially important, because Diderot did not view his emblems and hieroglyphs analogically but rather saw them literally as images of nature registered and reflected by the mind. Although the notion of the emblem was clearly available to him from the traditional emblem poetry which Scève exemplifies, Diderot used it in a different way. He focused on words and on relations behind words as consciousness perceived them.[8] For the deaf, imitative, acting gestures simultaneously represent meanings. Similarly, for poetry, words function like gestures, referring to objects while simultaneously depicting or enacting their meanings.

Diderot, consequently, defined poetic language through the paradoxical movement and stasis (in musical as well as pictorial rhythms) as hieroglyphs and emblems channel nature (or life) into art, mirroring as well as representing the poet's perceptions in new

---

[7] *Ibid*., pp. 377-78.

[8] Distinguishing *thought* and *expression*, Diderot wrote about poetic style: "There lives, then, within poetic discourse, a spirit which moves and enlivens all the syllables. What is that spirit? I have often felt its presence, but all I know of it is that it causes things to be spoken and represented at the same time, that at the very moment that hearing seizes them (the things), the mind is moved, the imagination sees them and the ear hears them, and that the discourse is no longer merely a sequence of forceful terms which present thought powerfully and nobly but composed of a tissue of hieroglyphs, massed one upon the other, which paint it. I might say, in this sense, that all poetry is emblematic." Diderot, p. 374 (trans. mine).

constellations. But while he sought to use these means to reconcile a sensibility nourished by his empiricist bias with his continuing search for formal values, he did not succeed. Later, he sought to reconcile acting as an imitation of nature with formal drama in his *Comedian's Paradox*—the very title testifying to his lack of success. For hieroglyphs and emblems, or the comedian's paradox, underscore that eighteenth-century paradox which has communicated itself to this day. By dissolving both the image and the consecutive function of language into states of mind, Diderot lost the stabilizing voice—of Amor, Wolf, and Goat—that would remove the poet's psychological involvement into a context where the embraced woman is actually, and simultaneously, *L'Idée*.

Immanuel Kant, in his way, supplied that voice by imposing at least an apparently objective order upon the material of consciousness. Although at the outset of his first critique, Kant, too, granted the empiricist premise that all knowledge is derived from sense experience, he created a set of mental structures in which all types of human activity from knowing to choosing to judging could be accommodated. Still locked into our consciousness, though capable of perceiving forms instead of flux, we can contemplate that formal, symbolic realm of art or poetry where our experience (the matter of "life" the poet takes to his art) is used to play with forms otherwise inaccessible to human knowledge. Kant, then, went a long way toward solving the paradox inherent in Diderot's emblems and hieroglyphs, but he did so by compartmentalizing all existence into separate, independent realms. True, as Murray Krieger made clear in his essay, "Fiction, History, and Empirical Reality," Kant created a phenomenologically determined order whose categories were drawn from the human mind and which therefore still reflected the order of the human mind as defined by the Age of Reason.[9] But Kant also did more: he described a universal structure of consciousness in which, however separated one from the other, an independently existing world of objects and ideas beyond the range of perceptual activity could be included. This model is useful not only within the confines of the *Critique of Judgment* but also as a general pattern for the functioning of poetry.

---

[9] "Fiction, History, and Empirical Reality," *Critical Inquiry*, 1, No. 2 (1974), 352-54.

IV

The eighteenth-century paradox may have been only partially solved by Kant, but the reverberations of his achievement are still felt today. For however unsatisfactory his particular terms may have proved to be, Kant (without in the least desiring it) built, in effect, a bridge from life to art without removing either artist or critic from his inner life or from his place as the measure of literary judgment. As the material defining the poet's existence was transformed into an independent world through the activity of the mind, the poet's life could truly become, with Wordsworth, the subject of an epic. But since his time, and Kant's, two alternatives have emerged from the eighteenth-century paradox: either poet and poem have been seen as fused or they have been separated by a distinct (physical or spiritual) reality—usually at the expense of the poet. The very relationship between the poet and his seemingly detached persona or mask in late nineteenth-century symbolism points out this duality in a deeply avant-gardist literary environment.

In this fresh encounter with an old paradox, a third example is provided by the theory of Paul Valéry. Valéry was intensely aware of this impasse: the more the poet focuses on his self, his consciousness, the more distant he becomes from that objective, rationally accessible whole which for him was the work of art. In his early treatise on the method of Leonardo da Vinci, however, Valéry in a sense reproduced Kant's architectonic achievement. Both the creative mind and the poet's art are viewed as *processes*, building and organizing an artistic form. Valéry called this process "abstraction." The artist's mind (like Leonardo's) is ordered (i.e., organized) and its contents rendered "abstract": "This abstraction is more or less energetic, more or less easy to define, to the degree that those of its elements which are taken from reality exist in more or less complex constellations." The mind, then, encompasses "the most expansive collection of forms . . . a crowd of beings, . . . of possible memories" and recognizes them through the *form* of its activity. [10] A relationship between the mind, the organization of the world, and the work of art exists, creating an order in which

---

[10]"Introduction à la méthode de Léonard de Vinci," in *Variété* (Paris: Gallimard, 1924), pp. 240-41. Translation mine. See also *Variety*, trans. Malcolm Cowley (New York: Harcourt Brace, 1927), pp. 252-53.

they all can cohere. But while this view might imply that poetic objects can be dissolved into mental states in poet or reader, Valéry drew back from these implications. He retained, strenuously at times, the literary object.

Valéry's poetic language takes its rise from the self—being occasioned by the moment of initial inspiration, the so-called *état poétique*. Unlike Diderot's emblems and hieroglyphs, however, it exists as a distinct unit, an existent with a world of its own that develops when "abstraction" or, as he calls it also, "construction" is imposed. Language, Valéry wrote in his famous essay, "Poetry and Abstract Thought," is "transformed into nonlanguage and then, if we wish, into a form of language differing from the original form." [11] It is part of the poet—Valéry likens the poetic universe to a dream world—but it is also distant from the poet, a transformed, organized, harmonious dream world. In another famous reference, he compares the poem to a machine producing effects in readers that approximate *états poétiques*. [12] But by calling it a machine (which takes a long time to build) and by viewing poetry in terms of his own unique universe, Valéry recognized that the artistic object—the poem—constitutes its particular world, its *emblem*, in which the materials of minds and objects are joined and transformed.

Consciousness and objects, as Valéry makes clear, are related to one another in new musical, as well as pictorial, harmonies. Their relationship mirrors the poet's attempt to come to terms with the physical world around him and to re-create himself, and the objects of his perception, within a new aesthetic whole. Favoring musical harmony, yet also being intimately aware of spatial relations, Valéry came closest to defining the nonverbal, harmonizing function of poetry when he described the dance. In "Dance and the Soul" body and mind are displayed in mutually distinct relations, one constantly displacing the other, yet each remaining itself. Valéry's Socrates comments at the end of the dialogue:

Doubtless, the unique and perpetual object of the soul is what does not exist; what was and is no longer; what will be and is not yet; what is possible, what is impossible—that is the soul's concern, but never *never* what is.

---

[11] Valéry, "Poésie et Pensée Abstraite," in *Variété*, V, 142-43. Trans. by Denise Folliot in *The Art of Poetry* (New York: Vintage, 1961), p. 65.
[12] Valéry, *Variété*, V, 151. Trans. in *The Art of Poetry*, p. 74.

And the body, which is what it is, see, it can no longer sustain itself in space. Where shall it bestow itself? Where shall it come into being? This One wants to play at being All. It wants to play at the soul's universality. It wants to remedy its identity by the number of its actions. Being a thing, it explodes into events.[13]

Relations of this nature, suggesting the dance of the mind among things and the dance of things among minds, are caught in the verbal dance of poetry. Towards the end of the dialogue Valéry sees the dancer—"that woman who once was there"— devoured by countless forms. Similarly, in a poem, the mind and its objects (including the body) and the language that passes between them are obliterated as they are absorbed into their specific poetic world. In the eighteenth century, Condillac distinguished between the *danse des pas* (the language of poetry) and the denotative *danse des gestes* (prose discourse). In the twentieth century, Valéry viewed the dance similarly as a paradigm for poetic language as its rhythmic harmony (through which body and mind interact) turns into an independent existent.

V

Valéry has shown that in a dynamic structure, poet and poem, persona and mask, depend on closely intertwined relations of mutually distinct entities. In other words, it is as important to save the literary object as it is to save the poet's life. To some extent, at least, Monroe C. Beardsley's and W. K. Wimsatt's "intentional fallacy" was surely prompted by their identification with an age in which the poet could safely disappear to preserve the independence of the poem. In fact, the "intentional fallacy" may never have been conceived were it not for the fact that since the eighteenth century the appropriate view of literature (no matter how objective or ostensibly "classical") was always refracted through a self and its highly self-conscious universe of discourse. In getting rid of the poet's self—and getting rid of the reader's as well—Beardsley and Wimsatt hoped to retain the aesthetic object as an end in itself. But if that procedure is found wanting, the opposite is equally

---

[13] "L'Âme et la danse," *Oeuvres*, II (Paris: Gallimard, 1960), pp. 171-72. "Dance and the Soul," trans. by Dorothy Bussy in *Selected Writings* (New York: New Directions, 1950), pp. 197-98.

difficult. If the literary object is eliminated, if Wimsatt is turned around, and all poetic activity is dissolved into mental contexts in which poet, reader, and work are merged, we return to the eighteenth-century paradox and stand to lose once more the communality of literature.

It is no coincidence, therefore, that our fourth paradigm will return us once more to the Kantian solution to the eighteenth-century problem in which an objective order is portrayed as an analogy to a structure of the mind. For one of the most crucial issues on which the resemblance of eighteenth- and twentieth-century poetics can be measured is that of the disjunction between subject and object on which the question of intentionality turns. The very issue on which the romantic sensibility asserted itself at the end of the eighteenth century was its need to include self and "other" in a single consciousness whose matrix and boundaries were those of the poem. This fact is useful to contemplate, not just because it explains the resurgence of taste for romantic literature, but also because it illuminates the role of the poet's intention—his conscious and unconscious acts in the composition of his poem—and the poetic process as a whole.

The various versions of phenomenological interpretations of intentionality, from Husserl and Brentano to Merleau-Ponty, Poulet, or in a very different way, Heidegger as well, share a similar stress on the role of intention viewed in a very special light. Curiously, intentionality, in a philosophical sense, reappeared in our vocabulary just as in a common-sense literary meaning it was being eliminated. But as the term in its technical sense became available, it seemed to provide a new perspective, helpful to an understanding of the epistemology of the literary imagination. For, while appearing to describe a mental process, intentionality as used in this system focuses on the interchange between two distinct terms. It prescribes a process of perception: the reciprocal relationship of subject and object *within* consciousness. It is easy to see how this way of viewing reciprocal relations in knowledge would appeal to critics seeking to retain both the mind and the object it re-creates. For the poem *qua* object constitutes precisely that mental context expressed in language which contains both the intending object (of perception) and the intending consciousness.

The idea of intention as employed by those critics concerned with the creative process (i.e., how the poet "intends" to convert life into art, consciously or unconsciously) and the same idea as used in phenomenological criticism are by no means unrelated. They share the analogy to the process of perception. Intention so defined is thus shifted from the poet's actual person to the mental context expressed in language; it becomes part of the objective tissue of the work which can be explained through the reciprocal tension between the intending poles. Intention in the common-sense meaning of the term, therefore, continues to be part of the poetic context; at the same time, its use in the technical phenomenological sense envisages its function as part of the texture of language. The problem of the New Criticism, in which the work is closed off from life, has been eliminated, yet the work as an independent entity may also have been preserved. This hybrid formalism, which allows the intrusion of intention through the objective process of consciousness, offers yet another solution to the "eighteenth-century paradox."

Our fourth example is drawn from Martin Heidegger's famous essay, "Hölderlin and the Essence of Poetry." [14] As a philosopher, and as a commentator upon poetry and poetics, Heidegger's manner of interpreting language is most useful to our purpose, because it sheds a fresh light upon *intention*. Heidegger sought to determine what is essential to poetry and at the same time to relate it to Being. Two of the quotations from Hölderlin used in this essay to illustrate the "essence of poetry" are pertinent to our discussion. The first is that language is the "most dangerous of possessions." The second is a quotation from a poem identifying our activity as a "conversation." In the first instance, Heidegger relates all language to existence: "Language has the task of making manifest in its work the existent, and of preserving it as such." It is dangerous, because, by its very presence, language presents us with the possibility of nonexistence. Hence its necessity and dangerousness are concomitants: since language is the one "possession" by which man is defined, it alone "affords the very possibility of standing in the openness of the existent." It therefore establishes the connection between man and life: it is "good for the fact that . . . man can *exist* historically." [15] Hence it is not a tool at man's

---

[14] This essay will be found in the anthology edited by Gras, pp. 27-43. For bibliographical details on anthologies cited in this essay, see Krieger's introduction. Further references will cite the editor's name and the anthology page number only. My thanks to my friend and colleague Richard Rorty for his helpful criticism.

[15] In Gras, p. 31.

disposal but "that event which disposes of the supreme possibility of human existence." Its danger is also its necessity.

Language so defined is not "actual," for it has to be realized in terms of the essence of what man actually is. When man in general becomes a poet and language in general becomes poetry, a conductor from consciousness to Being by way of the existent may have been found. Poetry, then, is the language of history and existence, its essence consisting in the fact that it transforms life in such a way as to give us a sense of Being. Here the crucial quotation stems from a fragmentary poem, "Reconciler, you who have never believed . . . ," which contains the phrase "Since we have been a conversation / And have been able to hear from one another." While man is defined by language, it is made actual only through conversation. Without binding speaker and hearer together, language is a potential but not an actual characteristic of man. But the conversation reflects more than a mere use of language. In conversing, mere man is becoming a poet, as language actualized becomes the language of poetry. For Heidegger points out that Hölderlin identified the conversant with the conversation ("we have been a conversation"). Moreover, since speaker and conversant are drawn together, theirs becomes a single conversation which is also implied in the curious phrasing that identifies "us" with the conversation we conduct. The actualizing of language thus turns the user of words into the word itself.

Finally, the conversation takes place in the perfect tense: "we have been a conversation," suggesting a continuity that extends from the past to the present. But the past the critic had in mind was located in two previous lines: "Much has man learnt. / Many of the heavenly ones has he named," since "we have been a conversation." [16] The single continuing conversation, then, has to do with man's learning and his naming of the gods. Language becomes actualized when it is continuous, when it transforms what we "are" into the conversation we conduct (and which we "are"), and when it perpetuates man's naming of the "heavenly ones," i.e., when it assumes all those characteristics by which poetic language is identified. Heidegger concludes: "Existence as a single conversation and historical existence—are alike ancient, they belong together and are the same thing." But language has existed since the naming of the gods and has been connected with knowledge.

---

[16] *Ibid.*, pp. 32-33.

Drawing from the fountain of man's knowledge, it realizes the function of poetry, for it turns man, and his world, into the words that are woven of the consciousness they share: "that it is precisely in the naming of the gods, and in the transmutation of the world into word, that the real conversation which we ourselves are, consists."[17]

The conversation as projected by Heidegger unites, then, not just speaker and listener and creates them in a new community; it is through the realized presence of the user of language as the language itself that language is "actualized" and turned into poetic language. This transformation of identities would not be possible without presupposing that they exist in a "structure of consciousness," however defined, in which language can function. Moments are picked out of "ravenous time" and are fixed in the word which, in turn, *is* man, the poet. Here the poet's life and existence *become* the poem precisely as "we" is verified as "have been a conversation." Heidegger extended Husserl's notion of intentionality to "incorporate the whole existence of man in its various modes" as a prereflective structure of consciousness.[18] Hence, the interplay of "we" and "world" and "word" also extends to the poet and the various personae he projects, all of whom are part of his consciousness and define his existence.

It may seem far removed from Hölderlin, but to complete our fourth paradigm it may be appropriate to test our conclusions by rereading the opening lines of Scève's *Dizain* XIV. The difference between the two poets, Scève and Hölderlin, is glaring, but there are also some parallels. Both poets searched for mythological equivalences of highly personal states; both wrote within prescribed conventions; and both met Heidegger's desire to examine the "essence" of poetry since both their works have come down to us as continuous poetics. But, most important, both poets projected their works as "conversations," i.e., as interactions of minds within a consciousness projected by their poems' language. In Scève's first two lines we have accordingly inferred a sensibility that interacts with other minds pictorially, dramatically, and theoretically:

> Elle me tient par ces cheveulx lyé,
> Et ie la tien par ceulx là mesmes prise.

---

[17] *Ibid.*, p. 33.
[18] See Gras, "Introduction," pp. 1-2.

> She holds me by this hair bound
> And I hold her by this same (hair) captive.

Typically, the image described by these lines functions through an interchange of subject and object—the pronouns *je* and *elle*. Two are caught in one image by means of a single rhetorical expression. If the mutual grasp of the hair, whose possessive is left ambiguous, is in any way suggestive beyond the obvious erotic allusion, it portrays a *conversation*, a learning, a moment of permanence snatched from "ravenous time." It also presents a play of opposing intentionalities within a single construct of consciousness, i.e., a form of perception. For the lovers' stance resembles first of all the pose appropriate to knowledge in which one beholds the other. Whether it occurs through the grasping of their hands or the vision of their eyes, both lovers (*je* and *elle*) are locked into each other and into the picture that combines them through the hold on the identical object. Visually, the image that comes first to the inner eye is that of the poet holding his lady's hair and being caught by it. But the poem begins with the pronoun *elle* and so calls this interpretation into question. By reversing the pronoun functioning as the subject in each line, by saying that it is *she* who holds *him* by the same grasp with which *he* holds *her*, the reciprocity and hence the mutuality of their grasp is established. Does she hold him because he holds her? Does he hold her because she holds him? Through this reversible question a synthesis is created which portrays the state of mind behind the image. It also combines two aspects of the self (functioning reversibly as subject and object). The figure thus portrays emblematically what is further elaborated in two succeeding images: the flame in which Amor wished to see them both devoured and the pit into which they are placed (to devour each other, reciprocally, as wolf and goat). For the fire of their endless fever could not yet be converted into the sacred flame—"Flamme si saincte . . ."—of Scève's final *dizain*.

There is a world of difference between Scève's somewhat crabbed Renaissance spirit and Hölderlin's density—though both are often obscure, their obscurities stem from different roots—but the relationship of intentionalities within a combining consciousness (Hölderlin's conversation in which "we . . . have been able to hear from one another") remains as their shared base. For Scève's Délie is not *any* object of perception (indeed, the poet is an "object" for her as well), but at the same time his conversant who, precisely as she occupies with him the poem's rhetorical figure and emblem, represents the image that turns the "world" into the "word."

Beyond Heidegger's interpretation, however, Scève's image is more widely instructive, for if we consider the intentionality implicit in his language in a phenomenological sense, we discover a further dimension. The idea of being mutually "hooked" is expressed through the lovers' grasp of the same object, the hair which, significantly, could belong to either. Indeed, it is the reversibility of their positions in relation to that object, functioning for each of the lovers in turn, that establishes it as the point of intersection of their consciousnesses. If each can project an intentionality in the act of knowledge, then the image, the emblem, and ultimately the language, portray their interactions and unify them. The route into the poem's interior, then, occurs by way of a mutually reversible action in relation to the hair which can be perceived by either. The posture assumed by this figure is that of perceiver and perceived; it is also that of mutual eroticism which is the point of the poem. Subject and object are therefore both separate and unified, for they exist in an identical realm of consciousness while reciprocally acting upon one another.

VI

For thinkers like Heidegger, "intentionality" in the widest sense points the way toward an understanding of the functioning of language in poetry. But even as it is used in a more restrictive sense, pertaining to perception, it suggests that the posturing of mind and objects (or other minds) can constitute the very relations by which language is defined and in terms of which it is re-created in poetry. In a poetic text we discern how a mind deals with its objects and confronts other minds, while remaining a single text in which all these relations are absorbed. It is through the use and understanding of perception that "intention" takes its place within the language of poetry. The poem's picture, emblem, or enactment of these inherent relationships indeed constitutes the poetic text itself.

The conversations, then, which we observed between minds and personae show that the use of the term *intentionality* in its phenomenological sense represents a shift in the function of intention from the poet's mind to the poem's words, i.e., to the consciousness embodied in the poem. But the question remains whether our fourth paradigm solves the problem posed by the eighteenth-century split between self-consciousness and poem any more than our first three examples. Indeed, part of the argument could be conducted on premises derived not from philosophy or linguistics, but from psychology and critical theory per se. Kenneth Burke, for example, in an early essay entitled "Freud and the Analysis of Poetry," applied Freudian principles to the exegesis of texts. His exposition, largely a reading of *The Rime of the Ancient Mariner*, involved two assumptions: (1) A poetic text is analogous to the human mind. Like the mind (which created it), the text exists on various levels; it uses devices like condensation and displacement to manipulate images of objects, other minds, and interior feeling-tones which texts, like minds, contain. (2) These manipulations are both pictorial and dramatic. Relations between minds and objects appear as images which exist in a state of tension with the unifying pressure of the text's language. In this view, too, mind and poetic object are telescoped in the identical text.

But if we abstract the implied relevance of the relations evident in the text to the lives and minds outside, classical statements of the Anglo-American New Criticism suggest similar recognitions. If, for example, we focus on the poem as an isolated text, we note that Cleanth Brooks's notion of the "functional metaphor" portrays precisely the dramatic tensions Burke had observed with the aid of Freud. It is only because it assumes evident relations between verbal levels and levels of consciousness outside the text that Burke's analysis, like the "intentionalities" of phenomenological critics, disturbs the dramatic picture of Brooks's "language of paradox." Thus, older theories like Burke's, as well as theories recently adapted from Merleau-Ponty to Poulet, from Heidegger to Staiger, create that hybrid formalism which allows the intrusion of intentionality through the objective processes of consciousness and hence offers a further solution to the paradox of eighteenth-century poetics. Only if the literary object is entirely eliminated, as has been evident in a significant strand of structuralist criticism, can this disjunction be overcome. But without the safeguards established in the concept of the romantic imagination (i.e., the poet's mind and his language fashioning by definition a distinct work of art), we do not solve the paradox. Rather, we kill the patient—the poem—instead of curing the symptoms that plague him.

Two recent anthologies of criticism—*European Literary Theory and Practice: From Existential Phenomenology to Structuralism*, edited by Vernon W. Gras, and *Issues in Contemporary Literary Criticism*, edited by Gregory T. Polletta—lead reader, critic, and student through an organized wilderness of present-day critical thought germane to our problem. Indeed, Gras's selections represent almost a model tour through changing notions of "intentionality" in theory and practice, because they reflect distinctly the changing attitudes towards the poetic process through which minds and texts are defined.

If W. K. Wimsatt banned "intentionality" from his temple of poetry, he did so because he believed in the inviolability of the poetic process. It was the "relevance" of the sixties that questioned this principle for the first time since it had gained ascendancy twenty years before as a new sophisticated doctrine. Under this pressure Wimsatt reexamined his early essay on the "Intentional Fallacy" published with Monroe C. Beardsley in 1945. In that later reconsideration, "Genesis: A Fallacy Revisited" (1968), which along with the former article is reprinted by Polletta, Wimsatt reviewed his earlier position in the light of the challenges he had encountered since the original paper had appeared. Among these, in particular, was phenomenological criticism which had grown in importance precisely because it seemed to solve the problem of the formalist isolation of the poem from life without abandoning the inviolability of the poetic text. But if Wimsatt proposed emendations they were all but unnoticeable, for neither the phenomenological reading, nor a revived interest in the relationship between the poet and his persona or mask, modified his view that any reading involving intentions on any level is exclusively biographical. Wimsatt even criticized the early Eliot, and therefore, by implication, Valéry, for the role he assigned the poet in "Tradition and the Individual Talent." He recognized what has often been overlooked: that Eliot's view of the poet's function and of the "objective correlative" are modern "hybrid formalism" as well, based on a version of the romantic imagination. Wimsatt squarely reaffirmed the position that the transmutation of mind into art, of poet into persona, are subjects of biography and history, and therefore cannot be considered within the context of criticism. [19]

---

[19]In Polletta, pp. 255-77. For facts of publication, see footnote 14.

Vernon Gras's selections, even more than Polletta's, lead the reader to an understanding of alternative solutions proposed by French and German philosophers and critics, while implicitly making clear why they eventually took hold in American criticism as well. As we read each selection, whether by Heidegger or Sartre, Poulet or, ultimately, Lévi-Strauss and Barthes, we begin to see why their theories have become increasingly influential. All of them touch upon the relationship between the poet's mind and the poetic text or act. And all of them gradually pushed against the rigid walls which formalist critics of the forties and fifties had erected between art and life. In phenomenological criticism (even in its restatement by Heidegger) the uniqueness of the literary text is retained. In fact, we particularly noted in Heidegger's essay how he sought to proceed from his consideration of language in general (language is the "most dangerous of possessions") to poetic language ("since we have been a conversation") in reaching Being. But in structuralism, as we know, the literary object itself is called into question. Most structuralist theories, therefore, reach beyond Coleridgean romanticism (to which in our analogy with the late eighteenth century they would correspond) toward that view of imagination which dissolves *all* art into life, and language, in general. In my view, Valéry's poetic (unfortunately omitted from both selections), i.e., the solution proposed in our third paradigm, comes closest to that middle ground between Wimsatt and Barthes which presents at least one answer to our problem. For by defining the poem through the *état poétique* instantaneously present to the poet, evoked in the reader, to be elaborated into a separately existing poetic form, Valéry may have done for *our* version of the eighteenth-century paradox what Kant had done for *his*.

VII

I hope I have shown the basic problem posed by the concentration upon the self since the eighteenth century: the need to illuminate the work through the mind of the poet to whom we owe its existence, but the equivalent need to retain the literary object as a formed entity with properties of its own—what Kurt Koffka called its "demand characteristics." Only then can we rest at peace and be sure that as the poet dons his disguises before his public, he re-creates, sometimes before our very eyes, a new work. Only then can we be confident of a communal experience that transcends his person and his poses even as he requires them for a fuller understanding of the poetic life. Like Stevens' Peter Quince, or like Mallarmé's Faun, but also like those intensely self-conscious characters in Woolf, Joyce, or Beckett, they confront themselves in the mirrors of their worlds transformed into infinitely distant, yet infinitely intimate forms. The man or woman who brings up children, reads the newspaper at breakfast, and falls in and out of love, is transformed into the aesthetic persona which represents, as it embodies, the work of art.

Index

Abrams, M. H.: on language, 59

Absurdist criticism: defined, 17; historical background of, 21, 110; questions posed by, 22; on language, 22, 86–88; on literary text, 88, 93–94, 95, 106; on privileged reader, 89; on civilization, 95–96; as dualistic, 110; mentioned, 105, 108

Academic criticism: Reductivist attack on, 98; mentioned, 99

Adams, Hazard: critical theory of, 12–17; on signifier and signified, 14, 16; on poetic language, 14–15; as Normal critic, 17; as Inflationary critic, 18; on structuralism, 31; mentioned, 7, 42

Adorno, Theodor, 97

Allegory: as critic's tool, 15; romantic concept of, 66; in poetry, 69–70; and symbolism, 70–71; de Man's view of, 78–79; mentioned, 74

American criticism: French influences on, 35, 37; and *nouvelle critique*, 55; mentioned, 158. *See also* Anglo-American criticism

Anglo-American criticism: international influences on, 35–37; pragmatism of, 71–72; Romantic Movement in, 80; mentioned, 156. *See also* American criticism

Anthology. *See* Critical anthology

Anthropology: history of, 118; and primitive religion, 128; contemporary neutralization of, 128–29

Antimyth: defined, 61; mentioned, 67. *See also* Mythology

Aquinas, Thomas, 78

Aristotle: on tragic hero, 135; mentioned, 78, 110, 137

Arnold, Matthew, 96, 98

Artaud, Antonin, 37

Auerbach, Erich: contemporary interest in, 35; critical method of, 41–42; and functionalists, 43; mentioned, 9, 50

Bachelard, Gaston, 55

Balzac, Honoré de, 49, 54

Barthes, Roland: as functionalist critic, 8; as Absurdist, 17, 87; critical theory of, 20, 36; his "Structuralist Activity," 56; on positivism, 56–57; on literary text, 88; on naturalizing culture, 94; mentioned, 9, 35, 36–37, 39, 41, 94, 104, 106, 158

Bataille, Georges: as Absurdist, 17, 86; critical analysis of, 52; literature defined by, 90; mentioned, 37, 94, 106

Bate, Walter Jackson: on literary influences, 46; on literary history, 48; mentioned, 10, 47

Baudelaire, Charles Pierre, 60

Beardsley, Monroe C.: his intentional fallacy theory, 149–50; mentioned, 157

Beckett, Samuel, 159

Benjamin, Walter: critical methods of, 41, 97; mentioned, 9, 36

DATE DUE